net.sex

net.sex

Nancy Tamosaitis

Ziff-Davis Press
Emeryville, California

Copy Editor	Jan Jue
Cover Design and Illustration	Regan Honda
Book Design	Lory Poulson
Word Processing	Howard Blechman
Page Layout	Tony Jonick
Indexer	Carol Burbo

Ziff-Davis Press books are produced on a Macintosh computer system with the following applications: FrameMaker®, Microsoft®Word, QuarkXPress®, Adobe Illustrator®, Adobe Photoshop®, Adobe Streamline™, MacLink®*Plus*, Aldus®FreeHand™, Collage Plus™.

If you have comments or questions or would like to receive a free catalog, call or write:
Ziff-Davis Press
5903 Christie Avenue
Emeryville, CA 94608
1-800-688-0448

ISBN 1-56276-285-0

Manufactured in the United States of America
10 9 8 7 6 5 4 3 2 1

ACKNOWLEDGMENTS

There is something really special about writing the first sexually oriented book that Ziff-Davis Press has ever published. It takes a tremendous
level of courage for a computer book publisher to commit to a serious
look at sexuality on-line. Thanks go to the courageous and smart Cindy
Hudson and her talented staff, including the insightful editor-in-chief
Cheryl Holzaepfel and her eloquent copy editor Jan Jue, Eric Stone
(may he live well and prosper :-#), and Margo Hill, who slaved day
after day helping with the most laborious aspects of the on-line survey
taking. Thanks also go to the talented sales and marketing team, including Juliet Langley, Genevieve Ostergard, Cindy Johnson, Lori
Koehlinger, Curt Johnson, Trina Tripoli, and Robbie Robinson.

Extra special thanks go to the visionary Mike Edelhart, my devel-
opmental editor, who single-handedly transformed the initial book
idea from merely being my meandering mealtime chatter to a real live
published book. I guess that means I owe *you* dinner now! ;)

I also would like to extend a heartfelt thank you to the *Computer
Life* editorial and marketing team, including editor-in-chief John Dick-
inson and features editor Victoria Von Biel for selecting a book excerpt
to run in the magazine, and to the enterprising marketing and public
relations staff, including the talented marketing director Vickie Welch
and her energetic and resourceful team: Laura Beraut, Simon Tonner,
and Laura Lawless. And thanks to Betsy MacKrell for the much-needed
support, and for taking the time to read the advance pages and offering
valuable feedback.

Special thanks are in order for Dr. June M. Reinisch, author of
The Kinsey Institute New Report on Sex (St. Martin's Press, 1990 hard-
cover, 1994 trade paperback), now Director Emerita of The Kinsey Institute, for granting permission to use the Kinsey Sex Knowledge Test
on the Internet for this book.

Tony Dubitsky, Ph.D, was instrumental in analyzing the results
of the on-line Kinsey Sex Knowledge Test. Rhonda Knehans-Drake was
invaluable in her assistance in creating the methodology behind the on-
line survey technique. Colleen Kilcullen, my best friend of 26 years and
impeccable editor and natural born proofreader (among many other
fine qualities), was a godsend in providing last minute, round-the-clock
editing assistance.

Thanks to Phillip Robinson—BTW, my personal pick for the
best-looking journalist in the computer field ;)—for giving me my start
in this authoring business and for being such a great, wise, and insightful friend.

Thanks to my parents for their love and support.

And last, but certainly not least, love and kisses to the ever-patient
and supportive SO—Ron Thompson—who over the past six months
has seen me go from "wired" to tired! <CLICK> That's the sound of my
modem hanging up...as I attempt to catch up on RL.

Introduction

There are over 10,000 Internet Usenet newsgroups and less than 200 are related to sex in any way. So why is this book devoted to net sex?

Sex talk means something different to everyone, and everyone has their own cerebral sexual toy chest of turn-ons and turn-offs. And almost everyone holds certain areas of sexuality in contempt while venerating other zones as secret treasures. While one person may be revolted by the notion of a man dressing up in heels and pantyhose, another finds delight in the concept. Yet another person would never admit to liking transvestitism in person, but lives a transvestite-positive life on-line.

Our parents and grandparents most likely came to grips with their sexuality in the back of a Chevy. Today's wired generation logs onto the Internet and quietly fumbles with their digital lover's buttons in the #hottub channel on the Internet Relay Chat, or perhaps in a closet in LambdaMOO, or through a slow, steady seduction of words posted on Usenet's alt.sex.

The Internet, which draws people from all over the world from every walk of life (except unwired), includes every possible sexual variation under the sun from "Leave It to Beaver" to "The Outer Limits." For many on-line people, pillow talk goes easier while nestled in the comforting, yet physically distant, arms of cyber-cushions.

net.sex was written for people who are curious about the wealth of sexual diversity available on-line, who may or may not have access to the Internet or a modem, but who are eager to learn who and what is really getting turned on besides the computer's power switch.

This journey also takes you to the *Kinsey Institute Sex Knowledge Test,* where you'll see how the Internet population fares on questions about sexual behavior and mechanics. The off-line population Kinsey polled several years ago failed. Does the Net population pass the test? *net.sex* marks the first time the adult-oriented factions of the Internet have been the subject of a professionally tabulated, fully on-line poll.

I can't claim this book covers every sector of sexuality on the Internet. Because the Internet is a fluid community, constantly reinventing itself and adding new layers upon layers, a book on any aspect of the Internet can never be truly definitive. However, thanks to the multitude of fascinating and wildly intelligent and insightful people I have met on-line while re-searching this book, I guarantee that *net.sex* will cast illuminating insights about the people frequenting the red-light districts of the Internet.

@>--/--\----
Love and Cyberkisses :-X,
nancyt7043@aol.com

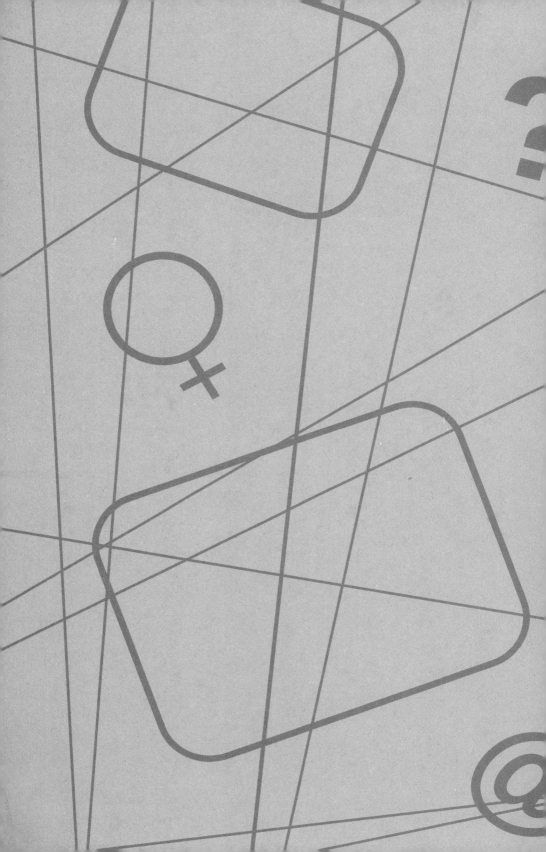

Where is the love?

Sex and technology go together as well as peanut butter and jelly—or do they? Is there something perverse about logging on to the Internet (Net) to find a sex partner, to download erotic photos, or to learn more about an esoteric sexual practice? Are the people who use the Internet as a source of sexual enlightenment, excitement, or entertainment dealing from a full deck? Do Net surfers who ride through the red-light district of the Internet ever travel to the mainstream G-rated districts of cybertown?

Is there a lot of "cybersex" happening on the Internet? And just what is cybersex, anyway? As the term is new, its definition is still evolving. Some use the word "cybersex" to encompass any material available on your computer—from X-rated images, games, movies, and stories to the erotically charged "one-handed typing" banter that involves two willing live participants typing in real time. However, when an Internet denizen posts a request for "cybersex," generally he or she is looking for a partner to exchange erotic e-mail with, or to meet live for steamy sessions on the IRC (Internet Relay Chat) area.

Some men and women believe the best type of sex is with a beautiful, willing partner and no commitment. That is what happens every time a person has cybersex. You can imagine what the digital lover looks like, and how he or she will sound and act. And you don't even have to make them breakfast the next day. "I don't think that cybersex will ever take the place of real sex, but it can almost satisfy for the time being," states "Mavrick." "The most important thing about cybersex is that you can be open, tell your emotions, and the other person really gets to know what really turns you on."

"Ron," a 25-year-old single father, looks forward to his nightly cybersex encounters because they give him "great insight into the workings of the female mind." His success "with women, at least in meeting them, and making it to the bedroom has been abysmal the last few years." Ron adds, "Once I'm in the bedroom, I have absolutely no problem, but I'm always looking for insights into women's thoughts and pleasures in hopes that I might again find that woman who'd like to have me in her life."

I decided to explore the red-light district of the Internet because I was looking for answers to the questions just outlined, and the notion of "virtual" strangers exchanging intimate thoughts and photos was intriguing to me. What I found was a substantial love onion; no matter how many layers of lustiness I peeled away, there was always another layer, fresh and original, just below the surface.

When I told Internet-savvy friends that I was writing a book about the sexual side of the Internet, they expressed concern. "Is there really enough to fill a whole book about?" they asked. Yes! There are countless socially and sexually driven nooks and crannies on the Net, from the ever-expanding Usenet newsgroup forums, to the bustling IRC channels, to the Multi-User Dimension (MUD) games that involve active fantasy role-playing. *net.sex* allows you to ride shotgun as I travel through erotically and socially driven digital terrains. Even most diehard Net enthusiasts tend to frequent only their favored areas, wearing digital blinders, unaware and unconcerned about 95 percent of what is available. I sought to peel away as many of the Net's layers as possible in an effort to get at what constitutes sex on the Net.

The Internet gets a lot of heat from the media about the easy, uncensored availability of erotica of all kinds. I wondered if exposure to so much information made the Internet population smarter about sex. To find out, I sent thousands of Internet denizens "The Kinsey Institute's Sex Knowledge Test." The results of this survey are in Chapter 2.

So, take a deep breath, jump into the passenger seat, strap yourself in, and come along with me on my journey through the red-light district of the Internet. Originally limited to only four computer systems, the Internet now consists of approximately 35,000 linked networks providing information on everything from where to find the finest transsexual hookers, to debates about the original *Star Trek* series versus *Star Trek: The Next Generation*, to Penn Gillette's fan club. The Internet was established in 1968 by the U.S. Department of Defense to keep communication lines open in the event of a nuclear war. But soon a new subculture of electronic communication evolved. Members of this digital society, concentrated in academia and the federal government, exchanged private messages. Then there came public "Net News" messages grouped by subject matter into "newsgroups." The Lewis and Clarks of this world, even now for the most part under 40 years old, can remember when reading everything in every newsgroup took barely ten minutes per day.

In the past few years, discussion about the Internet has snowballed. The Net is now regularly discussed in popular publications and on network television news and feature programs. Approximately 30 million people worldwide directly participate in the Internet, with one million new users signing on monthly. The daily volume of writings contributed to what is now called "Usenet" is rapidly approaching a hundred megabytes.

What is not so widely acknowledged by on-line enthusiasts such as Vice President Al "Information Highway" Gore and media executives, is that an impressive amount of traffic on the Internet is sexual in nature, with a small part of the Net devoted to taboo areas of sexuality such as bestiality and pedophilia. Since no one owns the Internet, and there are no governing bodies overseeing its content, there is no censorship. However, the same thing cannot be said for many of the commercial on-line services offering Internet access. While a sense of anarchy is the Net's trademark, commercial services are making distinct Big Brother overtures to their client base. For example, CompuServe and America Online insist that all subscribers abide by their "terms of service" agreements that forbid vulgarity and profanity. Prodigy has a "George Carlin-dirty-words-you-can't-utter-in-cyberspace" filter that weeds out objectionable language.

It seems whenever sexuality enters the mix, controversy soon follows. Debates over obscenity issues rear their ugly heads. *The Washington Post* reported in November 1994 that Carnegie Mellon University is eliminating all sexually oriented Usenet newsgroups from its computer network. Mike Godwin, staff counsel for the Electronic Frontier Foundation, a civil liberties and policy group devoted to on-line issues, is vehemently opposed to the university's censorship. "The Supreme Court has long held that, at least in theory, freedom of the press applies as much to the lonely pamphleteer as it does to the editors of a major urban daily newspaper. But the Net puts this theory into practice. The Net holds the promise of being the most democratizing communications medium in the history of the planet, and it is vital that we prevent the fearful and the ignorant from attempting to control access to it."

Other universities and institutions have wrestled with the problems created by sexually explicit materials on-line. Stanford University, Penn State, Iowa State University, and other schools have attempted to limit access to adult areas in varying degrees.

The prosecution and conviction of a Milpitas, California–based adult bulletin board operator (not directly affiliated with the Internet) for images downloaded in the Bible Belt, raises fundamental questions about federal obscenity law and free-speech protection in the computer age. Ironically, a Memphis-based hacker was the catalyst for the obscenity conviction of the adult bulletin board, Amateur Action. On the prowl for adventure, the hacker broke into the members-only California–based board, downloaded some hard-core photos, and then complained to local authorities about the content of some of the board's 20,000 photos, which included images of unclothed children at nudist camps, along with bestiality and assorted other verboten images. In July 1994, Robert and Carleen Thomas were convicted in a Tennessee federal court of transmitting obscene pictures over state lines via their computer bulletin board.

What are the ramifications of applying local community standards in federal prosecutions? The road has been paved for allowing the country's most conservative areas to have a disproportionately larger influence than appropriate, with the influence to dictate what sexually explicit words and images are allowed access to even the private, members-only side roads of the information superhighway.

FAQs and Other Newbie Netiquette

Before posting on any of the Usenet newsgroups, it is highly recommended that you first take a look at the group's FAQ (frequently asked questions) post. If you're a Net neophyte, or "newbie," you'll undoubtedly be tempted to ask questions that have been covered thousands of times before. The FAQ will, most likely, provide a comprehensive answer to all newbie questions. However, not all of the adult-oriented newsgroups mentioned in this book have an FAQ. Some of the newsgroups are simply too new, and don't have a handle on what all of the newbie questions will be yet. Others just don't feel like creating one. There is no NetGod on Usenet demanding that an FAQ be created. If a group does have an FAQ, they usually post it within their newsgroup at least every other week. FAQs for hundreds of Usenet newsgroups can also be found in alt.answers and news.answers.

By taking the time to see if there is an FAQ, you'll be following Usenet "netiquette," the etiquette rules that have developed over the years to let members of the on-line community peacefully interact. By following netiquette, you'll be less likely to suffer the burns set by "flamers." A flamer is an incendiary on-liner who delights in inciting trouble by chiming in whenever possible with derisive commentary. However, often a flamer personality just likes to watch other people's posts go up in smoke, so no manner of fire prevention can guarantee an on-line inferno won't erupt. Nonetheless, it never hurts to "lurk" around a newsgroup for a few weeks before posting, in order to thoroughly familiarize yourself with the lay of the digital land. A lurker is a digital voyeur who loves to watch but never participates. Some people remain lifelong lurkers. I subscribe to the theory that it is far better to have posted and lost than never to have posted at all. Half of the fun is seeing what comments will be generated by your post.

Flaming runs rampant all over the Internet, but it appears to be more flagrant and determined on the sexually oriented newsgroups. It often seems no matter what is said, there is someone out there who will pick a nasty bone of contention with it. However, some Usenet denizens like Paul Black attempt to pacify. In response to a rash of sexually smug posts, where some people were belittling others for their preferences, he stated that he "wished we could see less of the judgmental attitudes. If someone doesn't like one thing and someone else does, what is it to you? Some of you are flaming (shaming) others for what they do or do not prefer. Let it go. How are people supposed to share their sexuality— which is one of the most vulnerable areas of ourselves—when they get consistently slammed for it?"

Here is an example of a "form letter" flame one resourceful Internet denizen created in response to a man's advertisement for his singles dateline. Advertising is a definite no-no on the Net, and offenders are flamed unmercifully.

The Internet Usenet contingent is *extremely* class-conscious. Status is not measured by the number of dollars in the bank, or the type of car parked in the driveway. Address is everything on the Net—digital address, that is. Often it is not the words that are being measured, but the address. People who have the nerve to post to Usenet from America Online (AOL), Delphi, or Fidonet are often treated with scorn and contempt. The major commercial on-line services have only recently made Usenet accessible to their member base. Therefore, many of the members are unschooled in netiquette and generally make a lot of basic newbie *faux pas*, which generate resentment and impatience from the more experienced members of the Usenet society. The same post can illicit respect or disrespect depending upon where it originated.

However, the majority of people calling in from the newer Internet sites are no different from Internet veterans, and quite often, are one and the same. Many folks have accounts with a variety of services and usually just tap into what is available at that moment, or what is more economical to use.

It is illogical to make stereotypical assessments of the many thousands of users who reside at each digital post. For example, the following post was from "Ernie," and originated from his university account. "I have a big problem and was wondering if anyone else suffers from this affliction. I live in a van down by the river, and on my way to school each morning, I pass by this lake where the ducks are swimming. I have fantasies about putting hunks of bread around my dick and waiting for the ducks to nibble it off." If that post had originated from AOL, it would have been charcoaled with flames. As it came from a university Internet site, the worst treatment Ernie received was: "Having worked with a duck in a stage production, I can tell you that you do not want it anywhere near a body part as sensitive as your dick. They bite. It hurts. Don't do it."

~

To take part in exploring the Internet firsthand, all that is required is a computer, a modem, and an open mind.

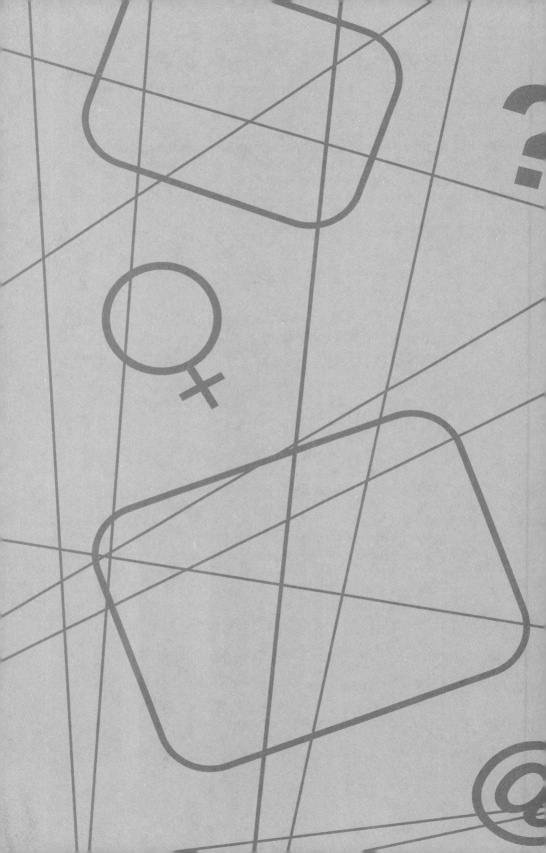

The national on-line sexual
knowledge survey

Like a lot of Americans, I read the results of the Kinsey Institute's National Sex Knowledge Test and was alarmed that the majority of respondents failed the test. Given to a nationally representative group of 1,974 Americans a few years ago, the Kinsey Institute test is comprised of sex knowledge questions, not invasive questions about personal sex habits. Respondents were queried on general areas such as sexual development, frequency of specific sexual behavior, and aspects of sexual reproduction such as pregnancy prevention. How could Americans *not* know the answers to these basic questions?

The Internet often gets a lot of heat from the media and society's conservative factions as being the bed of indecency, uncensored talk, and immorality. However, what is often not acknowledged, outside of on-line circles, is the vast international dissemination of timely and valuable information on a seemingly unlimited variety of subjects, including sexual knowledge. One Internet friend of mine states that the best way to provoke an answer to a question is to post a fallacy. Other people, armed with the accurate information, will immediately jump in and post the correction.

As sex and variations on a sex theme are discussed in approximately 200 active Usenet newsgroups on the Internet, I wondered if all of this talk was hitting home. Would the denizens of the sex-oriented Usenet newsgroups pass the Kinsey Institute Sex Knowledge Test? I also wondered how common were on-line sexual activities (e.g., "hot chats") among Internet users, and added five questions exploring this area. I decided to survey a random sampling of general Internet e-mail addresses found in the *Internet White Pages* book. During September and October 1994, over 4,000 tests were disseminated on-line.

The primary objective of my research was to determine whether there are statistically significant differences in sexuality knowledge between the general population and those who are on-line computer service users. A secondary objective was to determine if those who post to the on-line sexually oriented Usenet newsgroups have statistically significant differences in sexual knowledge compared with the general population polled in the original Kinsey Institute survey, and with those who are general on-line computer service users. A final objective to the study was to understand differences in claimed on-line sexual behavior between general on-line users and users of the on-line sexually oriented areas of the Internet.

This chapter written by Nancy Tamosaitis and Tony Dubitsky, Ph.D., with contributions from Rhonda Knehans-Drake.

Research Method

Using research on sexual knowledge within the general population as a benchmark[1], the same questions were put to the following two sample groups:

Sample Group 1   General on-line users with Internet e-mail addresses

Sample Group 2   On-line users who have posted one or more times to an adult-oriented Usenet newsgroup. E-mail addresses were pulled at random predominately from one of the most popular Usenet newsgroups, alt.sex.

Since some insights on the nature of on-line usage as it relates to sexual attitudes is required to understand the differences between Group 1 and Group 2, additional questions were asked. Due to the nature of the questions, and the desire to minimize the bias that asking these questions might introduce, Group 1 and Group 2 were further split as follows:

- Sample Group 1 survey A (Kinsey study—unaltered)
- Sample Group 1 survey B (Part of Kinsey study plus five on-line-related questions)
- Sample Group 2 survey A (Kinsey study—unaltered)
- Sample Group 2 survey B (Part of Kinsey study plus five on-line-related questions)

Surveys A and B are both found later in this chapter.

Rationale

This design provided flexibility and balance as respondents were obtained in each group, with a total of 739 respondents to the Kinsey questions. Group 1 in total and Group 2 in total were combined to analyze each group's relative difference in sexual knowledge as defined by the Kinsey study questions.

Finally, Group 1.B and Group 2.B were compared on those additional questions to determine how the impact of the interaction on a specific on-line service has altered sexual attitudes.

This design provided a wide range of information to explore, and the opportunity to understand the sexual knowledge differences between the general population versus the two tiers of on-line users.

Results

This study is the first published examination of any kind of the sexual knowledge of on-line users. In total, 4,000 surveys were sent out, and 739 completed surveys were received. Response rates were moderately high, with 316 usable questionnaires received from the general on-line users and 423 from the adult-oriented Usenet posters.

It should be emphasized that we embarked upon this survey fully cognizant that the on-line world was in itself a self-selected sample which constrains the projectability of these results to the population at large. Specifically, one limitation of any survey from a self-selected sample is that those who have not responded to this questionnaire may be systematically different from those who have.

∾

On-line Groups Scored Higher than the General Off-line Population Polled

- As shown in the following figure, on-line users achieved significantly higher[2] grades than the general population, with each of the on-line groups earning a significantly higher proportion of A's, B's, and C's than the general population.

- The general population polled by the Kinsey Institute received a significantly higher proportion of D's and F's than the two on-line groups.

- Overall, the on-line groups scored two full grade-points higher than the Kinsey sampling. The average grade for the two on-line groups was a C (averages for both general on-line and adult on-line samples were 12.4), while the average grade for the general population (scored by Kinsey) was an F (average = 7.9).

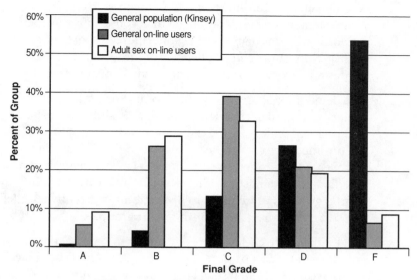

Kinsey National Sex Knowledge Test grades

I had anticipated that the adult-oriented newsgroup respondents would score higher than the general on-line users. However, this was not the case. By and large, there were few differences in the overall grade distribution for general and adult sex on-line groups:

- General and sex-oriented newsgroup respondents obtained virtually identical scores on the Kinsey test (averages were 12.36 and 12.42, respeciively; this difference is not significant).

There are several explanations for differences we observed in sex information knowledge between the on-line and off-line groups. While the Internet itself offers a variety of educational groups to the curious user, it would be naive to conclude that the more accurate sexual knowledge of the on-line groups is primarily attributable to self-education. The following competing hypotheses should be considered:

- As shown in the following table, there are marked demographic differences between the general population and the on-line user groups. Compared to the general population, both on-line user groups skew toward being upscale educationally and economically, as well as male, young, and single.

Additionally, both on-line user groups are more bicoastal than Midwestern, more politically liberal than conservative, and less traditionally religious than the total population. In short, the greater sophistication and open-mindedness of the two on-line user groups may account for their higher sex information test scores.

• The demographic profiles of the two on-line user groups were remarkably similar, especially for religious affiliation, region, and political philosophy. If there are any differences at all, adult sex on-line users tend to be slightly younger than on-line users in general. Consequently, since age is a key demographic variable that drives a host of other demographic variables, the former group is more likely to be single and currently enrolled in college than the general on-line user group.

• Finally, the relatively low scores shown by the general population could be an artifact of time. The Kinsey study was conducted several years ago, when social consciousness and media attention to AIDS and safe sex were not as omnipresent as currently.

Group Demographic Profiles

	General Population (Kinsey)	General On-line Users	Adult Sex On-line Users
Gender			
Male	48	85	82
Female	52	14	17
Age			
18–29	23	44	62
30–44	35	46	30
45–59	18	7	7
60+	24	1	1
Education			
No HS diploma	21	1	1
HS graduate	34	1	3
Some college	45	23	44
College graduate	0	74	51

Group Demographic Profiles (Continued)			
	General Population (Kinsey)	General On-line Users	Adult Sex On-line Users
Income			
<$15K	20	9	17
$15 to 24.9K	17	9	15
$25 to 34.9K	19	13	14
$35K+	27	66	50
Race			
White	80	88	85
Black	11	2	2
Hispanic	6	2	2
Other	1	6	10
Marital Status			
Married	60	35	26
Single	20	54	62
Separated/Divorced	10	7	11
Widowed	10	1	1
Religious Affiliation			
Protestant	49	15	15
Catholic	31	8	15
Jewish	3	10	7
Other	8	17	19
None	8	47	39
Political Philosophy			
Conservative	42	13	17
Moderate	32	30	37
Liberal	23	48	37

Group Demographic Profiles (Continued)			
	General Population (Kinsey)	General On-line Users	Adult Sex On-line Users
U.S. Region			
Northeast	22	25	30
Midwest	26	15	17
South	33	12	18
West	19	46	33

∽

Off-line Respondents Outscored the On-line Population on Three Questions   While the two on-line user groups significantly outscored the off-line population on most of the individual test items, the off-line population performed approximately as well as or better than both on-line user groups on the following three questions, all of which were true/false items. (The correct answers to these and other questions appear in this section. If you want to take the test first, go to the end of the chapter where the questionnaires and the correct answers can be found.)

Teenage boys should examine their testicles ("balls") regularly just as women self-examine their breasts for lumps.

The off-line population (with 73 percent accuracy) scored at approximately the same level as the general on-line user group (with 70 percent accuracy). However, the adult sex online user group significantly outscored both groups by a small margin with 78 percent accuracy. One explanation for this finding is that the sexually oriented Usenet newsgroups frequently disseminate important medical preventative tips, possibly accounting for the higher accuracy of this faction.

Menopause, or change of life as it is often called, does not cause most women to lose interest in having sex.

The off-line population (with 70 percent accuracy) scored as well as the adult on-line user group (with 68 percent accuracy) on this item. However, scores from the off-line group and the adult on-line user group were significantly lower than those for the general on-line user group (with 81 percent accuracy). This was an unexpected result, since we assumed that the young people who comprise many of the Internet groups would have little knowledge of or interest in menopause.

Problems with erection are most often started by a physical problem.

The off-line population (with 35 percent accuracy) significantly outscored the two on-line groups on this question. The general on-line group (with 18 percent accuracy) outscored the adult-oriented group (with 14 percent accuracy).

The Kinsey Institute discovered that this was one of the few questions that older and widowed Americans outperformed all the rest on. "Compared with all other age groups, twice as many people over 60 knew that most erection problems are physical in origin while the youngest age group was least likely to know this."

The Internet population is primarily young and well-educated. Young people are generally not overly concerned with erection difficulties, and being well-educated, they often read that psychological problems may factor into impotency.

～

Two On-line Groups Outscore Off-line Population   In general the on-line groups showed significantly more accurate knowledge than the off-line population on true/false questions pertaining to AIDS, safe sex, and homosexuality.

A person can get AIDS by having anal (rectal) intercourse even if neither partner is infected with the AIDS virus.

The Kinsey Institute's original survey revealed that 50 percent of the general population surveyed believed that the AIDS virus could be transmitted through anal intercourse even if neither partner was infected with the HIV virus. Conversely, 94 percent of the general on-line population and 91 percent of the adult user group answered correctly with "false," demonstrating their knowledge that one has to *have* the HIV virus in order to infect a partner.

There are over-the-counter spermicides people can buy at the drugstore that will kill the AIDS virus.

Only 5 percent of the survey respondents Kinsey polled answered this statement correctly as "true." However, 40 percent of the general on-line users and 31 percent of the adult on-line users answered this statement correctly.

*Petroleum jelly, Vaseline Intensive Care lotion, baby oil, and Nivea are **not** good lubricants to use with a condom or diaphragm.*

Half of the original Kinsey study survey respondents (50 percent) knew the above statement was true. Eighty-five percent of the general on-line users and 87 percent of the adult on-line users also saw the veracity of this statement.

More than one out of four (25 percent) of American men have had a sexual experience with another male during their teens or adult years.

According to Kinsey Institute data, "at least 25 percent of all American men have had a sexual experience with another male as teenagers or adults." While only 21 percent of Kinsey's polling sample selected the correct answer, 62 percent of the general on-line users and 58 percent of the adult sex on-line users chose the correct answer.

It is usually difficult to tell whether people are or are not homosexual just by their appearance or gestures.

Fifty-nine percent of the American adults Kinsey originally polled answered this statement correctly, choosing "true." However, according to *The Kinsey Institute New Report on Sex,* those who answered "false" to this item were "predominately conservatives and moderates, people living in the South, those who did not graduate from high school, people living in households with incomes less than $15,000, and older people."

Not surprisingly, the on-line population, comprised predominately of college educated people in the over $35,000 per annum bracket, scored very high with this item: 88 percent of the general on-line users and 84 percent of the adult sex on-line users answered correctly.

A woman or teenage girl can get pregnant even if the man withdraws his penis before he ejaculates (before he "comes").

The majority of Kinsey respondents, 65 percent, were aware that the pre-ejaculatory fluid which sometimes appears on the penis during sexual arousal may be potent enough to impregnate a female, even without ejaculation. However, an astonishing 94 percent of the adult sex on-line users and 92 percent of the general on-line users selected the correct response as well.

The on-line population fared significantly better than the general population on the following female-related items as well, suggesting that the male-dominated on-line world is very much interested in female sexuality issues:

Out of every ten American women, how many would you estimate have had anal (rectal) intercourse?

Respondents had the choice of selecting answers ranging from less than one out of ten to more than nine out of ten as the correct response. The correct answer, according to the Kinsey Institute data is three to four out of ten, that is, 30–40 percent of all American women have had anal intercourse. Nearly 80 percent of the general public Kinsey polled got this question wrong. The on-line population scored significantly higher with approximately 35 percent of the on-line groups answering correctly.

Out of every ten American women, how many would you estimate have masturbated either as children or after they were grown up?

Respondents had the choice of selecting answers ranging from less than one out of ten to more than nine out of ten. The adult sex on-line users scored significantly higher (46 percent correct) than both the general on-line users (34 percent correct) and the general population (18 percent correct).

Most women prefer a sexual partner with a larger-than-average penis.

Only four out of ten Americans the Kinsey Institute polled knew that, according to Kinsey data, most women don't have a preference for a sexual partner with a larger-than-average penis. However, seven out of ten Internet users (both the general on-line user and the sex group user) answered correctly.

∼

Both On-line Groups Scored Similarly   Both the general on-line user group and the sex on-line user group scored remarkably similarly in the Kinsey Institute Sex Knowledge Test. On an item-by-item basis, there were only a few significant differences between the two on-line user groups. Specifically, the two user groups showed significantly different scores on only five of the 18 test items. Adult sex on-line users were significantly more accurate than general on-line users on the following three items:

Teenage boys should examine their testicles ("balls") regularly just as women self-examine their breasts for lumps.

Seventy-eight percent of the adult sex on-line users and 70 percent of the general on-line users knew the answer to the above statement was true, compared to the general population's accuracy rate of 73 percent. The sexually oriented Usenet newsgroups frequently disseminate important medical preventative tips, possibly accounting for the higher accurate response rate generated by this faction.

Out of every ten American women, how many would you estimate have masturbated either as children or after they were grown up?

Respondents were offered responses ranging from less than one out of ten to more than nine out of ten. According to the Kinsey Institute data, "60 to 80 percent of females have masturbated." The sex on-line user groups come closest to the mark, guessing that 40 to 50 percent of all females have masturbated compared to the general on-line user groups correct response rate of 34 percent and the general population with only 18 percent accuracy.

What do you think is the length of the average man's erect penis?

Respondents were offered options ranging from 2 inches to 12 inches in assessing the length of the average man's erect penis. According to the *Kinsey Institute New Report on Sex,* this is one of the most popular questions asked by men writing to the Kinsey Institute. "The Kinsey research indicates that the average erect penis measures five to seven inches in length." An astonishing 95 percent of the adult sex on-line users, and 90 percent of the general on-line users, answered this question correctly compared with a general population accuracy rate of 60 percent.

General on-line users were significantly more accurate than adult sex on-line users on the following five true/false items:

A person can get AIDS by having anal (rectal) intercourse even if neither partner is infected with the AIDS virus.

Ninety-four percent of general on-line users and 91 percent of adult sex on-line users correctly answered "false" to the above statement.

There are over-the-counter spermicides people can buy at the drugstore that will kill the AIDS virus.

Forty percent of general on-line users and 31 percent of adult sex on-line users correctly answered "true" to the above statement.

It is usually difficult to tell whether people are or are not homosexual just by their appearance or gestures.

Eighty-eight percent of the general on-line users compared with 84 percent of the sex on-line users correctly answered "true" to the above statement.

Problems with erection are most often started by a physical problem.

This is the only Kinsey question that the general population scored higher on than the on-line sampling! While 35 percent of the general public realize that erection problems can be frequently attributed to a physical problem, only 14 percent of the adult on-line sex users and 18 percent of the general on-line users answered this statement correctly!

Interestingly, although the vast majority of on-line respondents were male, they appear to be more knowledgeable about women's sexuality than about their own. They know more about women and penis size, pregnancy during menstruation, females and anal intercourse, and females and masturbation. We can hypothesize that perhaps these are men who are driven by a deep fascination with women, and they tap into the on-line world to feed that fascination in a way that social encounters can't or don't.

*Menopause, or change of life as it is often called, does **not** cause most women to lose interest in having sex.*

Eighty-one percent of the general on-line user group compared with only 68 percent of the adult sex on-line user group answered this statement correctly with "true," compared with a 70 percent general population accuracy rate. The Internet Usenet newsgroups that deal with sexuality frequently attract young people, often of college age. It makes sense that they have little knowledge about or interest in menopause.

~

Age of First Intercourse   Respondents had the option of selecting from 11 years of age or younger incrementally to 21 years of age or older. Consistent with the Kinsey study, the majority (that is, over half) of each of the on-line groups were likely to underestimate rather than overestimate the age of first intercourse. Apparently, the Kinsey respondents as well as the on-line users tend to believe in the sexual precocity of youth!

As shown in the figure below, the two on-line user groups showed virtually identical performance on this item. There were no significant differences between the two on-line groups on the percent of respondents who were on-target, overestimated, or underestimated.

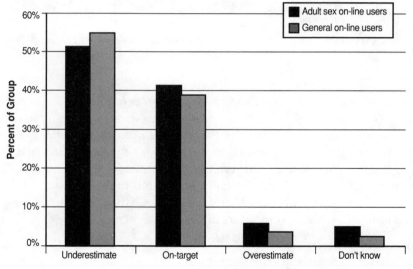

Accuracy of on-line groups: age of first intercourse

~

Frequency of Extramarital Affairs among Men   The general on-line group was significantly more likely to overestimate the prevalence of this phenomenon than adult on-line users, as shown in the following figure. The overestimation of the general on-line user group is in keeping with the results from the Kinsey study, whose respondents believe that extramarital affairs are far more common than they actually are.

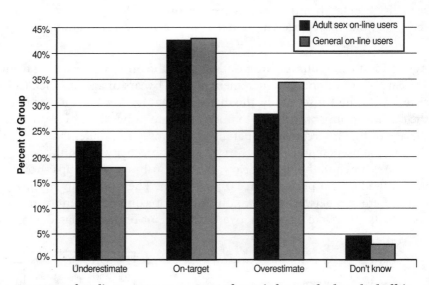

Accuracy of on-line groups: percentage of married men who have had affairs

≈

Heterosexual Anal Sex among Females   Also consistent with the results from the Kinsey study, both on-line user groups were more likely
to underestimate rather than overestimate the occurrence of this behavior. The response pattern shown in the following figure suggests that
people are still reluctant to believe that those other than homosexual
men engage in anal sex. Additionally, for reasons that are unclear, the
adult on-line group was significantly more likely than the general on-
line user group to respond "don't know" to this item.

≈

Incidence of Female Masturbation   As shown in the following figure,
the adult on-line user group was significantly more likely to be on-target
than the general on-line group. However, consistent with the Kinsey
study, the on-target levels are still low (accuracy is less than 50 percent
for each online group), again confirming what apparently is a popular
belief—that female masturbation is taboo, forbidden, or unusual.

≈

Length of Erect Penis   In contrast to the Kinsey study, where respondents
were almost two times as likely to overestimate as to underestimate erect
penis size, virtually all of the respondents (90 percent or more) in each of

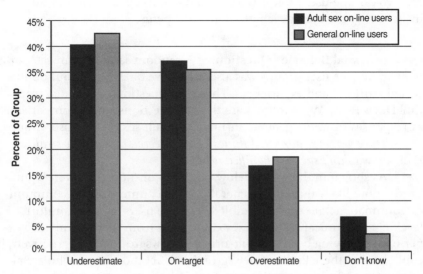

Accuracy of on-line groups: percentage of females having anal intercourse

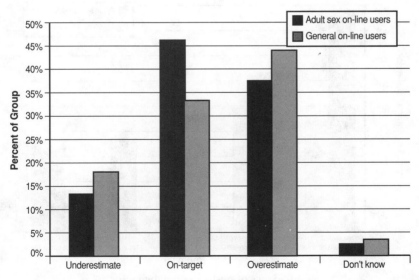

Accuracy of on-line groups: percentage of females who masturbate

the two on-line user groups were on-target in their estimates of 5–7 inches being the average length of an erect penis.

∼

On-line Sexual Behavior Questions   A random sample from each of the two on-line user groups was also asked five questions about online sexual attitudes and experiences. These five questions originated from Ziff-Davis Press. What follows are the five questions, and a comparison of responses from the general on-line and adult sex on-line user groups:

Have you ever admitted things (spilled secrets) to on-line strangers that you wouldn't say to a significant other?

As shown in the figure below, adult sex on-line users were significantly more likely than their general on-line counterparts to communicate intimate details on-line. Adult sex online users' greater comfort level in communicating about sex could stem from their cumulative experience of having been in adult-oriented newsgroups or, alternatively, it could be that these kinds of newsgroups attract individuals who are already at ease exploring such topics with others. At bottom, it's a "chicken-and-egg" question.

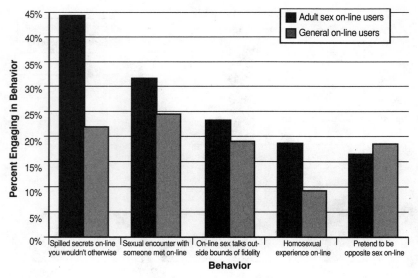

Incidence of on-line sexual behavior

	General Population (Kinsey)	General On-line Users	Adult Sex On-line Users
Question			
Women don't need regular gynecological exams	85	97	95
Teenage boys should examine their testicles	73	70	78
Menopause does not affect a woman's sex drive	70	81	68
Pregnancy is possible even with penile withdrawl	65	92	94
Erection problems are treatable	64	82	78
Length of erect penis	60	90	95
Can't tell who is homosexual by appearance	59	88	84
Women can get pregnant during menstrual period	51	62	65
People get AIDS through anal intercourse	50	94	91
Petroleum jelly and baby oil are not good lubricants	50	85	87
Females prefer larger penis	40	73	71
Erection problems are often physical	35	18	14
Age at first intercourse	25	39	41
Percent of married men having affairs	25	43	43
Percent of females who have had anal intercourse	21	35	36
25% of males have had a homosexual experience	21	62	58
Percent of females who have masturbated	18	34	46
OTC spermicides kill AIDS	5	40	31

Percent Correct Responses by Group

Assuming you are heterosexual, have you ever had a sexual-oriented on-line experience with a person you believed to be of your own sex?

Additionally, adult sex on-line users were significantly more likely than their general on-line counterparts to claim having had homosexual experiences on-line. This brings to light yet another "chicken-and-egg" question: Do adult-oriented newsgroups attract people who enjoy sexual experimentation or does the cumulative experience in such a group bring about a desire to try alternative sexual lifestyles?

Have you ever had an on-line experience where you pretended to be a person of the opposite sex?

Have you ever had a sexual encounter with someone you met on-line?

If you engage in sexually explicit on-line conversation, do you think this erotic on-line behavior strays outside of societal-acceptable fidelity boundaries?

There were no statistically significant differences between these two on-line user groups on any of the above items—pretending to be a member of the opposite sex on-line, having a sexual encounter with someone who was met on-line, and agreeing that on-line sex talk is outside the bounds of fidelity.

Conclusion

For the last several years, the media have been abuzz debating the essential character of the adult on-line areas. Are these PG-13, R-, and X-rated digital domains essentially cathouses, singles bars, or assignation dens? The results of the on-line Kinsey Institute Sex Knowledge Test, indicating that 73 percent of the respondents are single or separated/divorced, attest that the adult-oriented enclaves are, indeed, singles bars! The majority of the on-line respondents are in their 20s and 30s, affirming that this is where the young and dateless congregate on a Saturday (or any other) night.

Interestingly, the survey respondents were predominately bi-coastal. In fact, 63 percent of the on-line respondents reside on either the East or West Coast. Social trends frequently originate from both the East and West coasts, setting patterns for every significant social change in modern American history. Hence, what you see in Soho and Soma today, you'll see in Rockford in five years. So, middle America, brace yourself, as the popularity of sex on-line may soon be coming to a local Internet domain near you!

The survey demonstrated that both the sexually oriented and general on-line user group respondents are clearly more knowledgeable about women's sexuality issues than they are about comparable men's issues. Ironically, however, the vast majority of the respondents were male, over 83 percent. The on-line respondents clearly know more about women and preferred penis size, the possibility of pregnancy during menstruation, the number of women who have masturbated, and so on, but know much less about erections.

The on-line world is a self-selected sampling of humanity that predominately represents a bicoastal, young, male-dominated, highly educated, white, single, middle-to-upper class section of society who are unafraid of technology and are the trendsetters of tomorrow. Overall, the main impression I take away from the survey of the on-line world, including both the general and adult sampling, is that these people are not fundamentally different from the off-line world, just better informed about sexuality. And their privileged station in life—which includes the benefit of higher education and good incomes—makes it easier to learn more about *all* areas of life, including sexuality.

The Kinsey Sex Knowledge Test—Survey A

Ziff-Davis Press, with permission from The Kinsey Institute, is taking a look at how the on-line population's sexual knowledge compares with the results of Kinsey's off-line national study. Ziff Davis Press will be publishing the results of this survey next year. We look forward to your response to the Kinsey Institute's National Sex Knowledge Test.

1. Nowadays, what do you think is the age at which the average or typical American first has sexual intercourse?

    a. 11 or younger

    b. 12

    c. 13

    d. 14

    e. 15

    f. 16

    g. 17

    h. 18

    i. 19

    j. 20

    k. 21 or older

    l. Don't know

2. Out of every ten married American men, how many would you estimate have had an extramarital affair—that is, have been sexually unfaithful to their wives?

    a. Less than one out of ten

    b. One out of ten (10%)

    c. Two out of ten (20%)

    d. Three out of ten (30%)

    e. Four out of ten (40%)

    f. Five out of ten (50%)

    g. Six out of ten (60%)

    h. Seven out of ten (70%)

    i. Eight out of ten (80%)

    j. Nine out of ten (90%)

    k. More than nine out of ten

    l. Don't know

3. Out of every ten American women, how many would you estimate have had anal (rectal) intercourse?

    a. Less than one out of ten

    b. One out of ten (10%)

    c. Two out of ten (20%)

    d. Three out of ten (30%)

    e. Four out of ten (40%)

    f. Five out of ten (50%)

g. Six out of ten (60%)

h. Seven out of ten (70%)

i. Eight out of ten (80%)

j. Nine out of ten (90%)

k. More than nine out of ten

l. Don't know

4. A person can get AIDS by having anal (rectal) intercourse even if neither partner is infected with the AIDS virus.

True

False

Don't know

5. There are over-the-counter spermicides people can buy at the drugstore that will kill the AIDS virus.

True

False

Don't know

6. Petroleum jelly, Vaseline Intensive Care lotion, baby oil, and Nivea are not good lubricants to use with a condom or diaphragm.

True

False

Don't know

7. More than one out of four (25%) of American men have had
    a sexual experience with another male during their teens or
    adult years.

    True

    False

    Don't know

8. It is usually difficult to tell whether people are or are not
    homosexual just by their appearance or gestures.

    True

    False

    Don't know

9. A woman or teenage girl can get pregnant during her men-
    strual flow (her "period").

    True

    False

    Don't know

10. A woman or teenage girl can get pregnant even if the man
    withdraws his penis before he ejaculates (before he "comes").

    True

    False

    Don't know

11. Unless they are having sex, women do not need to have regu-
    lar gynecological examinations.

    True

    False

    Don't know

12. Teenage boys should examine their testicles ("balls") regularly just as women self-examine their breasts for lumps.

    True

    False

    Don't know

13. Problems with erection are most often started by a physical problem.

    True

    False

    Don't know

14. Almost all erection problems can be successfully treated.

    True

    False

    Don't know

15. Menopause, or change of life as it is often called, does not cause most women to lose interest in having sex.

    True

    False

    Don't know

16. Out of every ten American women, how many would you estimate have masturbated either as children or after they were grown up?

    a. Less than one out of ten

    b. One out of ten (10%)

    c. Two out of ten (20%)

    d. Three out of ten (30%)

e. Four out of ten (40%)

f. Five out of ten (50%)

g. Six out of ten (60%)

h. Seven out of ten (70%)

i. Eight out of ten (80%)

j. Nine out of ten (90%)

k. More than nine out of ten

l. Don't know

17. What do you think is the length of the average man's erect penis?

a. 2 inches

b. 3 inches

c. 4 inches

d. 5 inches

e. 6 inches

f. 7 inches

g. 8 inches

h. 9 inches

i. 10 inches

j. 11 inches

k. 12 inches

l. Don't know

18. Most women prefer a sexual partner with a larger-than-average penis.

True

False

Don't know

DEMOGRAPHIC CHARACTERISTICS

19. What is your sex?

    a. Male
    b. Female

20. What is your age?

    a. 18–29 years old
    b. 30–44 years old
    c. 45–59 years old
    d. 60+ years old

21. What level of education have you achieved?

    a. No high school diploma
    b. High school graduate
    c. Some college
    d. College graduate or higher

22. What is your annual household income?

    a. Less than $15,000
    b. $15,000–$24,999
    c. $25,000–$34,999
    d. $35,000+

23. What is your race?

    a. White
    b. Black
    c. Hispanic
    d. Other

24. What is your marital status?

    a. Married

    b. Single

    c. Separated/Divorced

    d. Widowed

25. What is your religious affiliation?

    a. Protestant

    b. Catholic

    c. Jewish

    d. Other

    e. None

    f. Don't know

26. What is your political philosophy?

    a. Conservative

    b. Moderate

    c. Liberal

27. Where do you reside?

    a. Northeast/United States

    b. Midwest/U.S.

    c. South/U.S.

    d. West/U.S.

    e. Outside U.S.

The Kinsey Sex Knowledge Test—Survey B

Ziff-Davis Press, with permission from The Kinsey Institute, is taking a look at how the on-line population's sexual knowledge compares with the results of Kinsey's off-line national study. We have also included some of our on-line-related questions as well. Ziff-Davis Press will be publishing the results of this survey next year. We look forward to your response to the Kinsey Institute's National Sex Knowledge Test.

1. Nowadays, what do you think is the age at which the average or typical American first has sexual intercourse?

   a. 11 or younger

   b. 12

   c. 13

   d. 14

   e. 15

   f. 16

   g. 17

   h. 18

   i. 19

   j. 20

   k. 21 or older

   l. Don't know

2. Out of every ten married American men, how many would you estimate have had an extramarital affair—that is, have been sexually unfaithful to their wives?

   a. Less than one out of ten

   b. One out of ten (10%)

   c. Two out of ten (20%)

   d. Three out of ten (30%)

   e. Four out of ten (40%)

f. Five out of ten (50%)

g. Six out of ten (60%)

h. Seven out of ten (70%)

i. Eight out of ten (80%)

j. Nine out of ten (90%)

k. More than nine out of ten

l. Don't know

3. Out of every ten American women, how many would you esti-mate have had anal (rectal) intercourse?

a. Less than one out of ten

b. One out of ten (10%)

c. Two out of ten (20%)

d. Three out of ten (30%)

e. Four out of ten (40%)

f. Five out of ten (50%)

g. Six out of ten (60%)

h. Seven out of ten (70%)

i. Eight out of ten (80%)

j. Nine out of ten (90%)

k. More than nine out of ten

l. Don't know

4. A person can get AIDS by having anal (rectal) intercourse even if neither partner is infected with the AIDS virus.

True

False

Don't know

5. There are over-the-counter spermicides people can buy at the drugstore that will kill the AIDS virus.

    True

    False

    Don't know

6. Petroleum jelly, Vaseline Intensive Care lotion, baby oil, and Nivea are not good lubricants to use with a condom or diaphragm.

    True

    False

    Don't know

7. More than one out of four (25%) of American men have had a sexual experience with another male during their teens or adult years.

    True

    False

    Don't know

8. It is usually difficult to tell whether people are or are not homosexual just by their appearance or gestures.

    True

    False

    Don't know

9. A woman or teenage girl can get pregnant during her menstrual flow (her "period").

    True

    False

    Don't know

10. A woman or teenage girl can get pregnant even if the man withdraws his penis before he ejaculates (before he "comes").

    True

    False

    Don't know

The following five questions are from Ziff-Davis Press. We welcome additional comments in addition to your yes/no responses. Please feel free to comment as extensively as you'd like.

1. Have you ever had an on-line experience where you pretended to be a person of the opposite sex?

    Yes

    No

2. Have you ever had a sexual encounter with someone you met on-line?

    Yes

    No

3. Assuming you are heterosexual, have you ever had a sexual-oriented on-line experience with a person you believed to be of your own sex?

> Yes
>
> No
>
> Don't know
>
> Doesn't apply, as I'm gay

4. Have you ever admitted things (spilled secrets) to on-line strangers that you wouldn't say to a significant other?

> Yes
>
> No

5. If you engage in sexually explicit on-line conversation, do you think this erotic on-line behavior strays outside of societal-acceptable fidelity boundaries?

> Yes
>
> No
>
> Don't know

DEMOGRAPHIC CHARACTERISTICS

6. What is your sex?

> a. Male
>
> b. Female

7. What is your age?

> a. 18–29 years old
>
> b. 30–44 years old
>
> c. 45–59 years old
>
> d. 60+ years old

8. What level of education have you achieved?

    a. No high school diploma

    b. High school graduate

    c. Some college

    d. College graduate or higher

9. What is your annual household income?

    a. Less than $15,000

    b. $15,000–$24,999

    c. $25,000–$34,999

    d. $35,000+

10. What is your race?

    a. White

    b. Black

    c. Hispanic

    d. Other

11. What is your marital status?

    a. Married

    b. Single

    c. Separated/Divorced

    d. Widowed

12. What is your religious affiliation?

    a. Protestant

    b. Catholic

    c. Jewish

   d. Other

   e. None

   f. Don't know

13. What is your political philosophy?

   a. Conservative

   b. Moderate

   c. Liberal

14. Where do you reside?

   a. Northeast/United States

   b. Midwest/U.S.

   c. South/U.S.

   d. West/U.S.

   e. Outside U.S.

Thank you for your participation.

Survey Answers

Note, each of the 18 Kinsey Institute Sex Knowledge questions (not including demographics or the five Ziff questions) counts for one point. So, the total possible number of points you could get is 18. Using this chart, score each item and then add up your total number of points. When a range of possible answers is correct, according to currently available research data, all respondents choosing one of the answers in the correct range is given a point.

Question Number	Answers
1	f, g
2	d, e
3	d, e
4	False

Question Number	Answers
5	Any answer gets a point
6	True
7	True
8	True
9	True
10	True
11	False
12	True
13	True
14	True
15	True
16	g, h, i
17	d, e, f
18	False

Notes

[1] June M. Reinisch, Ph.D, *The Kinsey Institute New Report on Sex.* New York: St. Martin's Press, 1990.

[2] Throughout this discussion, the term "significant" is used as a shorthand phrase to indicate that a difference between two or more groups is statistically different at the 90 percent confidence level or higher. In other words, the observed results are extremely unlikely to have occurred (less than 10 times in 100) due to chance or error. Other things equal, the observed results are attributable to differences between groups.

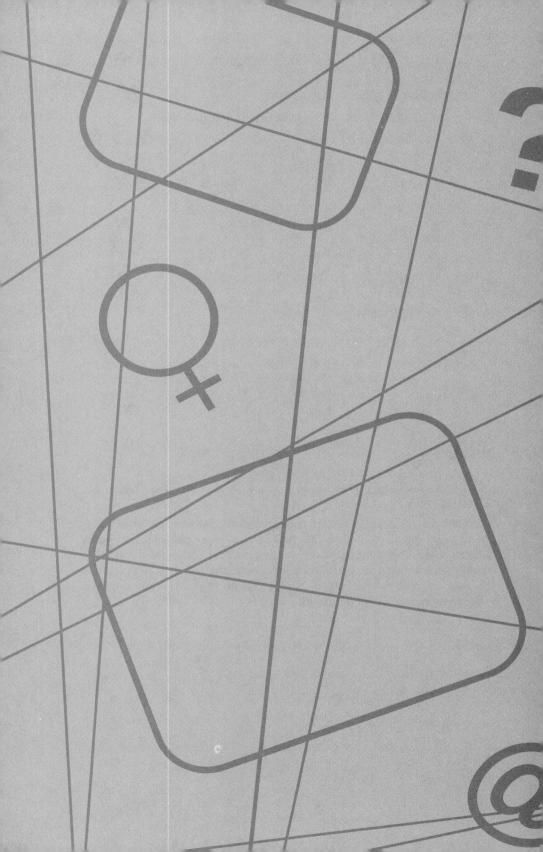

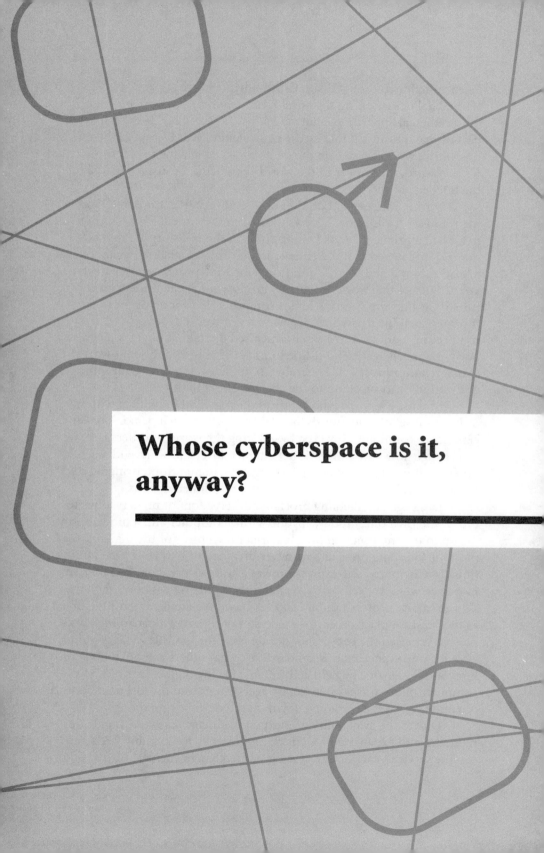

Whose cyberspace is it, anyway?

Science-fiction author William Gibson defined "cyberspace" as a "consensual hallucination" in his novel *Neuromancer*. Can we dismiss on-line life as ethereal apparitions that vanish when we log off? Is cyberspace a part of real life, or is it merely the equivalent of REM sleep? Is the on-line world, with its focus on the democratic, equalizing power of the written word, the answer to the world's problems, or just a panacea for the intellectual elite?

During my research on the social and sexual "game dens," "meeting rooms," "bedrooms," "news rooms," and "bordellos" of the Internet, I had a privileged look behind some of the Net's private digital doors. I discovered that the emergence of on-line–related sexuality raises a host of moral and legal conundrums for which we have no ready answers. The off-line world frequently grouses about the impersonal nature of on-line communications, grumbling that modems increase interpersonal insularity in a depersonalized world. Does on-line communicating lend itself to a disenfranchised digital nation, or a neighborly, global village? Can on-line intimacy lead to healthy, real-world sexual relationships? Is it preferable to initially fall in love with someone's mind or to succumb to the charms of the flesh?

Because everyone who ventures on-line is an individual with his or her own set of rules, needs, habits, and history, each person's on-line experience is unique. However, by entering the world of cyberspace, we *can* change how we communicate, interact, love, and work with each other off-line. This chapter reports from the digital front, bringing back news of love, lust, morality conflicts, and unfulfilled dreams.

Long ago A.J. Liebling proclaimed, "Freedom of press belongs to those who own one." Today, anyone with a computer and a modem can log on to the Internet and own his or her own piece of the digital press pie. Our founding press fathers never dreamed of a world where internationally distributed self-expression was as easy as pressing the Enter key. However, wherever self-expression travels, controversy is never far away. The obscenity prosecution of Milpitas-based Amateur Action BBS, billed as the "nastiest place on earth" as a result of files downloaded in Tennessee, has renewed the censorship debate issue for the '90s. Who is responsible for implementing the standards for what others can do and say online? Should anyone be held accountable for the digital distribution of computer photo images that depict everything from the girl next door to the nude girl next door going down on the neighborhood dog?

Due to the availability of inexpensive image scanners, rapid-fire modems, and expansive hard disks, the Internet, as do many BBSs and on-line services, carries GIF (Graphic Interchange Format) files or other varieties of graphic images with sexual content. These images can range from your standard *Playboy* magazine fare to esoteric sexual fringe practices such as up-close-and-personal scatology shots or photos depicting infantalism. The rapid growth of the consumer VCR market is frequently linked to the expansion in the adult video market. Similarly, this increasing availability of low-priced consumer computer technology has led to a rapid increase in GIF-file traffic. To keep their systems afloat, system operators who might never frequent an adult book or video store have either allowed or encouraged sexually oriented images to be exchanged on their systems.

Although most of the active Internet community rebukes censorship of any kind, the off-line world is clamoring to control what it views as a world without legal boundaries or a civilized form of self-policing.

This chapter explores many facets of the ethical, moral, and legal issues surrounding sex-related activities on the Internet through anecdotal experiences and via the voices of experienced Internet navigators.

Digital Love: Who Are You Really Romancing?

America is a country obsessed with the body beautiful. Today, female fashion models with the angular look of pretzel sticks are idolized by legions of aspiring waif wannabes. Madison Avenue and Hollywood tout America the Beautiful in the form of picture-perfect humans, prodding men and women to exercise away every last bit of body fat. However, beyond the brainwashed masses of humanity lies a reservoir of people who value content over packaging. For these people, the Internet is a playground of the mind, a welcome respite from a sanitized, commercial world.

A plea for body acceptance cross-posted in alt.support.big-folks and alt.romance brought two like-minded souls from different continents together. "David," a portly man living in Switzerland, was tired of being overlooked by women because of his size. Feeling demoralized and depressed over a bad breakup and hopeless that he'd ever meet someone who'd love him as he was, he attempted to lift his mood by attending a party. He states, "After attending an outdoor party, and seeing several women go after the 'stud/macho' types of men," he returned home to his terminal and released all of his "anxieties and frustrations onto the electronic newsgroup alt.support.big-folks." His post lashed out at womankind, proclaiming that they were all "looking for one type of man—solely based on superficial reasons." Although David received lots of hateful flame letters, "Lynette," a Midwesterner, was moved by his words.

She realized his words echoed her own sentiments and experiences with men. "I decided that this was a chance for me to prove to him that all women were not like that. I e-mailed him saying that I understood where he was coming from, and that if he needed someone to talk to, I was available," explains Lynette.

After a few exchanges of e-mail, a live "talk" session date was established. "We were logged on for over six hours that first night, talking about everything under the sun and comparing notes on romantic experiences, likes and dislikes," enthuses Lynette. The connection between the two was immediate. "It was almost scary," says David. "From that very first live chat session, we both felt like we had met our other half." The live talk sessions grew longer and more frequent, and led to phone calls. "We tried to keep the phone calls short because the money could be put to better use with airplane tickets," says Lynette.

Following an exchange of pictures and cassette tapes filled with each other's favorite love songs, the two were anxious to meet face to face. Hastily arranging a loan, David flew thousands of miles to meet Lynette at the Des Moines, Iowa, airport. The couple enjoyed a wonderful week together, immediately realizing that their feelings went well beyond friendship. Lynette journeyed to Switzerland over Thanksgiving break. As Lynette is an enthusiastic medieval history buff, the couple journeyed to Montreux to visit a castle. During their exploration of every nook and cranny of the castle, David whisked her away to a quiet corner, got down on one knee, and proposed marriage to Lynette. A fairy-tale happy ending in a fairy-tale medieval castle setting—all courtesy of the Internet.

David and Lynette's love story illustrates one of the most compelling virtues of on-line life—the value of substance over style. Words alone carry an innate power on-line. Words have the power to connect disparate souls from distant lands minus the weighty significances of physicality.

However, sometimes relationships, inspired and transported by ASCII text scrolling by on a computer screen, set up false expectations and illusions. Without the interference of day-to-day mundane reality, it is possible to portray ourselves on-line as matchless representations of humanity. It is just as easy to project perfection upon our digital love mates. We may never know if "Bob" leaves the toilet seat up, but we are moved by his mastery of the complete works of Shakespeare and his encyclopedic knowledge of post-Coltrane jazz.

Falling in love with a digital fantasy, rather than the real person that lives and breathes behind the monitor, is a common pitfall of net-inspired affairs. "Mike," a computer science student in Pretoria, South

Africa and a self-described "typical cyberjunkie," learned firsthand about the perils of projecting fantasy expectations onto a real-life person. Mike, someone who "prefers computers over people since they are a static system and react the same no matter what," was playing on a MUD named Ultimate, when a male friend introduced a new female friend, "Marta," from Germany. After the introduction, Mike's friend quickly whisked Marta away to a private area of the MUD so that no one could talk to her but him. A few weeks later, the digital pair broke up, and Mike provided a comforting electronic shoulder to cry on; a new friendship was forged. Marta fell in love with Mike through the supportive, caring words he typed and said she wanted to spend every available moment with him. "Not being 'all there' myself, I found her loving words felt really good. It felt great to have someone somewhere WANT to spend time with me...and not because they had to, but because they wanted to," explains Mike.

"Because of the two-dimensionality of this modem medium, people express sentiments that they would never say face to face, or at least so quickly into a relationship. In person, some things may not be expressed due to the circumstance or a swing in the conversation. In writing, however, you get all your feelings down like you feel them," Mike adds.

Mike, increasingly consumed by his relationship with Marta, spent all of his time in the computer lab talking to her. His academic performance suffered as he pined away for Marta at the keyboard. However, Marta, a Croatian native, graduated, and the digital pair lost contact. "Several months had passed since we had spoken, and I missed her a lot. I called her old dormitory and one of her friends gave me her new phone number. I phoned her, and she explained that the only way she could stay in Germany was to marry a German student. She explained that she married this student just for convenience, and that they were not sleeping together. She said that I was the only one she really loved."

For the following year, Mike phoned Marta two or three times a week, and the pair spoke for hours at each session. Finally, Marta started prodding him to travel to Germany to be with her.

Mike economized like crazy to save money for the trip but still didn't have enough money to go. Marta sent him some money, and he booked his travel plans. However, Mike's company did not want him to take a three-week vacation at that time. "I handed in my resignation," states Mike. "I just had to see her. Nothing else mattered.

"The first time I saw Marta in person at the airport, my heart almost stopped," swoons Mike. "I was definitely in love." Mike and Marta had a passionate affair. They tried to spend all possible time together when her husband was at work. Although Marta said she didn't love her husband, Mike could see that they shared a special kind of open relationship—"an understanding...something she didn't share with me. Suddenly the situation was much clearer, and I understood for the first time what I was doing," Mike said.

However, even with his ambivalence about the relationship, and its doomed outlook, Mike decided to move to Germany. His first weekend in Germany, Mike stayed with the couple and proceeded to get extremely drunk at the Octoberfest. "She took one look at me in this sorry, drunken, emotionally needy state, and said she never wanted to see me again.

"Now I'm living in a foreign country, unable to speak the native language, and the person who inspired me to come here doesn't even want to hear my name anymore," Mike says. "I'm still glad I came. I have lived and made it on my own, experiencing a new culture."

Still, he can't help but be a bit dour on the prospect of success with computer-initiated relationships. "In my opinion, any long-distance relationship that is started over the electronic medium is doomed to failure. There are just too many variables involved in the physical world that do not carry over to the two-dimensional world of the Internet. The Internet is not a substitute for the real world. It is just a beautiful representation of some of the better points of reality. When abused and perceived as reality, it can become an ugly mess. To all those people trapped in MUDs and IRC, spending all their time trying to make contact with people on the Net, I have only one message: 'Switch the damned terminal OFF and GET A LIFE!'"

However, some people view the Net as a way to get a life quickly. "Doreen," a 35-year-old homemaker, was appalled to learn about her husband's chronic infidelity. As a way of lashing back, she logged on to the Net's alt.personals forum and began answering posts from men looking to meet and/or converse electronically with women. "I live in a small Louisiana town, in the middle of nowhere, and there is no one here I'm interested in philandering with," Doreen writes. "My husband is a traveling salesman, and his pool of potential lovers is endless. I felt enormously betrayed learning about his infidelities, and I vowed to get even. However, thus far, I've kept all my relationships strictly on-line. I'm tempted to take the plunge, and meet someone off-line, but I feel like I've experienced a lot of the thrill of an affair, without the burdens and responsibilities it may entail."

"Rexxxxxxxx," an accomplished best-selling author who's been happily married for over 38 years, believes that "on-line sex is as close to real sex as two people can get because of the interactivity and real ecstasy each feels when they take the time to do it properly." His book *Modem Love* includes highlights of Rexxxxxxxx's separate encounters with eight women. Rexxxxxxxx says that each episode lasts from one to five hours each and is a blend of intimacy, romance, and passion. Are such on-line affairs violations of fidelity or just healthy fun? "I've been faithful to my wife during our wonderful marriage," states Rexxxxxxxx, "and our sex life is what many others strive for. When I do go on-line—where I'm anything but monogamous—I always keep my activity anonymous because of my marriage. I always say I'm married when asked, but I think the anonymity is a big part of the mystery and charm of cybersex.

"About half the women I meet are looking for a mate," states Rexxxxxxxx, "and the other half are looking for fun and games. If I were looking for a mate, I would not be anonymous. I notice that as cyber-relationships get closer, layers of anonymity strip away." The author's wife is aware of her husband's cybersex activities. "She does not care to know the details of my dates. She is confident that my on-line sexual escapades will remain on-line, that I have been a faithful spouse for 38 years, and grateful that our sex life has never been as rich, imaginative, and active as it is right now. I'm obviously learning as much as I teach in every cybersex session I engage in."

Will the lure of cybersex still entice Rexxxxxxxx after his manuscript is turned in? "Yes, I will still engage in cybersex, but much less frequently. Our sex life is infinitely richer as a result of my on-line sex. My wife says that I am a better lover than ever, and that I was an A+ before I went on-line. Deep down she knows my greatest passion in life is freedom and that my on-line behavior is a manifestation of that freedom. My only requirement is that no one ever get hurt, and nobody ever does. I guess another passion I have is to hurt no one under any circumstances."

While many men and women have the self-control to keep their on-line love affairs digitally grounded, others use the medium to physically meet new lovers. A 34-year-old Lincoln, Nebraska, man who goes by the on-line handle "Remmy" applies what he has learned through the Usenet newsgroups and through his countless on-line affairs to his married life. "My wife has long stopped asking me, 'Where did you learn to do that?'" said Remmy, a molecular biologist. "Rather she has accepted this new fount of information as a wonderful tool to enhance our lovemaking."

Remmy admits to having had scores of on-line lovers. However, the love and lust doesn't always stay on-line. Remmy shares every detail of his electronic tryst with "Tasha," a married 30-year-old clerical worker and mother of two. The play-by-play development starts with Remmy's post in alt.personals seeking a lusty e-mail pen pal. Tasha responds through an exchange of erotic dialogue. The e-mail starts out on an exploratory note. Tasha writes, "Although I despise crudeness like you, I am eager to learn more about my sexuality, and feel a sympathetic soul with you." The prose grows increasingly intimate through the ensuing two weeks. The pair moves from an anonymous mail site, to revealing their own actual e-mail addresses, to the exchange of photos, phone numbers, and addresses, to making plans to physically meet to consummate their passion—all in 14 days. The e-mail exchange that Remmy forwarded to me covers well over 100 pages and constitutes only a two-week digital courtship. Remmy enjoys the challenge, the thrill of wooing women through his artful construct of seductive prose. "You may hate me after reading how I operate," Remmy tells me as he proceeds to upload what he describes as the "true confessions of someone who uses the Net to exploit women and explore one's own sexuality in all the twisted forms the human imagination can conjure." In reality, it appears both parties are willing partners, and to cast stones at Remmy would be absurd.

"From the other side of a computer screen we have to interact on a completely different level," states Remmy. "I think that this makes this a genuinely unique way for people to become acquainted, since it demands we articulate our thoughts and dreams. I'm a romantic, so I truly believe this medium will have a lasting impact on how people relate to one another in coming years." Remmy, a bisexual, is addicted to the variety of women and men he can meet on-line. Occasionally overcome with guilt, he attempts to stay away from the social side of the Internet. Time after time, his willpower collapses, and he returns to draw new satisfaction from the digital well. "It is hard to keep a marriage fresh," Remmy explains. "No matter how hard you try, it all gets boring. The people I've met on the Net spice up my life significantly. And the variety is seemingly infinite. Some of the men and women I meet are only digital and phone friends. Others become physical lovers. Either way, the intensity I feel for them is genuine even if the relationships don't last very long."

Remmy says he is completely honest with anyone he meets on the Net. His post in alt.personals states that he's married and is not looking for sex, but would enjoy exchanging written erotica and fantasies. The women that respond to the personal ad are, according to Remmy, sexually savvy and don't understand why more women don't "open up." A level of trust is established and anonymous e-mail addresses are replaced by direct e-mail addresses. "Intensely stimulating discussions of sex follow," details Remmy. "An erotic aura envelopes both parties, and something more satisfying is always desired. Phone numbers, work and/or home addresses are exchanged, photos are sent back and forth. Soon, phone sex becomes the preferred contact mode. People do not generally find the coldness of the electronic love affair to be enough. We all need the voice, the image, the feeling of someone real caring for them."

Remmy admits that frequently his e-mail-inspired erotic experiences go beyond the phone and computer. "We'll sometimes reach the boiling point where a physical meeting is a necessary release for both of us. Sexual liaisons become established, and while some have been very mutually satisfying, others have not. When the physical side sours, so does the cyber side. Without exception, however, when the physical side is good, the cyber side is maintained and is wonderful, but simply not adequate alone."

Moralists and the popular media often like to paint the Internet as the digital den of iniquity. Remmy's experience could be twisted to convey that point of view. However, isn't it a mistake to blame the medium for the morality, or lack therein? Although Remmy has an endless source of new lovers at his fingertips through the Net, it's not the medium that's the catalyst, it's the people. Remmy could just as easily find an endless well of lovers through anonymous phone sex encounters or by placing personal ads in newspapers. It is simplistic to assign human traits of immorality to a web of servers. The complex web of humanity behind the servers is just that, a complex web, capable of an infinite array of actions and emotions.

Pastor K. Galen Greenwalt of the First Southern Baptist Church of San Diego moralizes in a recent article in the *San Diego Union Tribune* that digital social interactions are "nothing more than people being selfish. It's a sin. Sex is a holy bond of intimacy between a man and a woman who will be together for life. They are meant to share their bodies, not a machine." "GrimJim," a MUD aficionado offers a rebuttal: "The thing that ticks most Internet folks off is the sensationalism. The rants we read and see on mainstream TV about virtual sex and the Internet are all *way* out of proportion. Why aren't we hearing more about the raging phone sex market, and how we have to keep our kids away from the 1-900 lines? Conventional media interprets things only in terms of what they've previously known: gratuitous sex and violence. What has happened to the human element? Depth of analysis is so lacking these days."

However, some net-inspired liaisons are the stuff of Stephen King novels rather than Barbara Cartland romances. Many people harbor secret sexual fantasies. Often, these fantasies are never shared. Net interaction, with its lure of anonymity combined with the opportunity to exchange thoughts and ideas with people outside one's immediate social circle, can be the catalyst to live out one's most secret fantasies. "Bill," a

48-year-old Texas sheriff, wields a lot of power in his small Texas town. Nonetheless, in the deep recesses of his soul, he longed to be dominated by a woman. This secret was never revealed to his wife during their 22-year marriage. But in just a few months, he found himself revealing his most intimate fantasies to a total stranger he met on alt.sex.bondage, a Usenet newsgroup devoted to discussing the Dominance/submission (D/s) lifestyle.

Bill responded to a post from a woman asking about the proper use of handcuffs. He received a reply thanking him for the information. She then asked him a few questions about himself, which he promptly answered. After several messages back and forth, she asked Bill for his mailing address so she could mail him a photograph. "We ended up exchanging photos," recalls Bill. "She sent me a very provocative photo. She was dressed in a leather outfit that barely covered her crotch, boots up to her thighs, and wielding a whip! My poor middle-aged body started generating hormones as if I were a teenager again."

A few days later Bill received e-mail from her stating she'd received his photo and that he was exactly what she was looking for! Bear in mind, Bill admits to being overweight, balding, and not at all handsome, and she was only 25 years old. She suggested that they try playing a little D/s (Dominance/submission) via e-mail. "Somewhere all my common sense went out the window, and I agreed to be her e-mail slave!" says Bill. "I rationalized that this will just be a fun escapade, a little mental game where we talk dirty electronically to each other."

However, Bill soon discoverd that he was in digital water over his head. He agreed to obey the digital dominatrix's every command. At first her commands were simple and even health-oriented. She ordered Bill to cut down on cigarettes, leaving his smokes in the car, and only smoking during his lunch hour. She announced that she now owned his body, and Bill did as he was told. "I found myself sexually excited as I craved for a smoke, and suffered for want of one," recalls Bill.

Bill then received a package in the mail, which he was to keep on his desk and not open until she commanded him to do so. After several days, her call to action arrived in his e-mail box. He was to go to the office that night to open the package and bring a VHS camcorder and audio cassette player. Inside the package was an audio cassette. Bob inserted the tape into the player and was immediately mesmerized by her powerful, compelling, young voice. She told him to set up the video camera to record and to slowly undress. She then ordered him to open the inner package and remove the items. Inside was a leather collar and a small whip. She ordered him to whip his own backside 50 times. "I had welts all over my backside, and was in terrible pain," recalls Bill. "She then ordered me to masturbate until I was about to orgasm, but not to go all the way. Then she permitted me to cum, and commanded me to swallow my semen. After following her instructions to destroy her audio tape, I mailed the video, collar, and whip back to her."

A few days later Bill received e-mail from her "telling me that she was pleased with me and would keep me as her slave." Bill was overflowing with joy over her pronouncement.

Six months later, the dominatrix phoned Bill from a hotel three blocks from the station house. When he entered her hotel room, she instructed Bill to strip naked and fasten on a black leather collar. "She commanded me to stand with my feet apart with my hands on the back of my neck. She fastened my wrists together with leather cuffs, she cuffed my ankles together, and placed a leather blindfold on me. I became really scared, and as I tried to say something, she slapped me violently across the face." They proceeded to engage in very "violent" intercourse for many hours.

"I had no condom on, and became terrified that she had some terrible disease. Although I came there of my free will, this was not [consensual] sex. She did not ask, she just took," states Bill. In his blindfolded state, Bill recalls hearing the shutter clicks of a camera. Finally, she untied him from the bed and removed the blindfold. She pointed to his clothing and ordered Bill to get dressed and get out. "I don't think ten words were spoken during the whole encounter," remembers Bill.

A week later, Bill received e-mail from her. She told him that she wanted a blond-haired, blue-eyed baby. Her only reason for coming to town was to get pregnant. She did not know yet if she was, but she had a good feeling she was. Bill heard nothing from her for six weeks, and then received an e-mail stating he was free from slavery. She ordered him never to contact her or she would tell his wife all about them and include a few photos.

Few Internet-related experiences are so dramatic and bizarre. Nonetheless, it brings new ethical issues to light. Do sexual conversations that occur on-line encourage irresponsible intimate acts in the real world? And is virtual infidelity a sin? Did Bill the sheriff go over the proverbial moral line as soon as he started exchanging e-mail with his digital dominatrix, or only after a physical act was consummated? Or are all moral attitudes to be personally interpreted, and if an individual has an interest in an area, and it doesn't harm anyone else, is it acceptable?

Lily Burana, editor-in-chief of *Future Sex*, a San Francisco–based magazine that explores sex, technology, and culture believes that morally, there is no difference between sex on-line and sex in the real world. In a recent interview with the *San Diego Union-Tribune*, Burana says, "Is it ethical to do a gender swap (a woman pretending to be a man on-line or vice versa) or distort your age? For me, the jury's still out. If you never meet the person, never talk to the person over the phone, then what's the harm? Still, it's hypocritical to say that we can shrug off our social expectations about appearance everywhere except the bedroom," adds Burana. There are no easy answers to the moral and ethical questions raised by the possibilities of the on-line world. However, we can be sure that the debate will sustain itself into the next century.

The Internet has been the catalyst for more than one *Same Time, Next Year*-type scenario. "Cindy," a happily married professional in the software industry, met "Bob," another happily married computer professional, through Cindy's post on alt.personals. "I was lonely and looking for a friend I could share my problems with," Cindy explains. "Bob and I talked openly and easily and eventually progressed to sharing things about our married lives. Mostly we found we were happy, but wished we could have X, Y, and Z. We found that we had a lot of complementary 'needs.'"

The conversation stayed on-line for months until one day Cindy walked into her office to find a long-distance call on hold. "Bob told me he was being sent to California for a trade show and wondered if we might be able to meet there. It so happened that I also attend this trade show every year, so I went and we met. I wouldn't say it was 'love at first sight,' but there was genuine fondness and mutual attraction. I struggled with the concept of a one- or two-night stand and was thrilled when Bob's parting words were 'It's time to return to our separate lives, but there will be other trade shows...'"

With an estimated 25–30 million people on the Internet, the experiences are bound to be wide and varied. The only definitive conclusion to be drawn from the anecdotal experiences relayed in this chapter is that the Internet is an avenue for people to converge, exchange ideas and information, and explore tapped and untapped aspects of their personalities. The experience of sharing ideas, erotic expression, and fantasies through the modem medium is safe and incredibly stimulating for many people. However, if your goal is to deliberately deceive and hurt others along the journey on the new information superhighway, what has really been gained? Is the new, deceptive persona preferable to the genuine personality, or will this digital deception slowly erode your self-esteem and confidence? I believe these are questions each individual must answer.

However, it is too often the case that the adult-oriented portions of the Internet are turned into freak show fare to satiate mass media's ravenous appetite for endless amounts of sex and sensationalism. "Brian," an MIT student, states, "I think the American public is not accustomed to the notion that the Internet offers a place where people from all over the world can engage in the free exchange of ideas on sensitive topics such as human sexuality. It is all too easy to dismiss such alternative discourse as the ravings of a bunch of 'sickos.'"

The Internet is an electronic representation of everything that is available off-line, simply offered under a digital roof. There are good, bad, and indifferent people circulating on the Net, just as exist off-line. To paint the Internet as featuring only one hue, one canvas, one artist, and one subject is to create an imposter portrait. "The moral system" of the Internet "is like a document written in alternate ciphers which change from line to line."[1] The only constant we *can* count on is change.

Legal Issues on the Electronic Frontier

Mike Godwin, legal counsel for the Electronic Frontier Foundation, advises users of electronic networks about their legal rights and responsibilities, and instructs criminal lawyers, law enforcement personnel, and others about computer civil liberties issues. (For information on EFF mailing lists, newsgroups, and archives, mail eff@eff.org. To browse EFF's archives, use ftp, Gopher, or WAIS to connect to ftp.eff.org, gopher.eff.org, or wais.eff.org respectively. Look in /pub/Eff. To get basic EFF info send a message to info@eff.org. Send detailed queries to ask@eff.org. For membership information, mail membership@eff.org.) I turned to him to learn more about the myriad legal issues concerning sex-related on-line activity. Authorities have been trying to define what's obscene and what's not for years. Attempts range from "I can't define it, but I know it when I see it," to hundreds of judicial rulings. The question can be daunting. Godwin, in his *Internet World* article "Sex and the Single Sysadmin," helps us sort it out with this definition:

> In lay terms, a jury (or a judge in a non-jury case) would ask itself something like these four questions:
>
> 1. Is it designed to be sexually arousing?
>
> 2. Is it arousing in a way that one's local community would consider unhealthy or immoral?
>
> 3. Does it picture acts whose depictions are specifically prohibited by state law?

4. Does the work, when taken as a whole, lack significant literary, artistic, scientific, or social value?

If the answer to all four questions is "yes," the material will be judged obscene, and it will be constitutional to prosecute someone for distributing it. (It should be noted in passing the pictures of the "hardness" of *Playboy* and *Penthouse* photography have never been found to be obscene; their appearance in digital form on Usenet sites may create copyright problems, but they won't create obscenity problems.)

As Judge Richard Posner comments in the October 18, 1993, issue of *The New Republic,* "Most 'hard-core' pornography—approximately, the photographic depiction of actual sex acts or of an erect penis—is illegal," even though it is also widely available. (Let me emphasize the word "approximately"—Posner knows that there are countless exceptions to this general rule.) That is, distribution of most of this material is prohibited under state or federal anti-obscenity law because it probably would meet the Supreme Court's test for defining obscenity.

But what precisely is the Court's definition of obscenity? In *Miller v. California* (1973), the Court stated that material is "obscene" (and therefore not protected by the First Amendment) if (1) the average person, applying contemporary community standards, would find the materials, taken as a whole, arouse immoral lustful desire (or, in the Court's language, appeals to the "prurient interest"), (2) the materials depict or describe, in a patently offensive way, sexual conduct specifically prohibited by applicable state law, and (3) the work, taken as a whole, lacks serious literary, artistic, political, or scientific value.

This is a fairly complex test, but most lay persons remember only the "community standards" part of it, which is why some system operators are under the mistaken impression that if the material is common and available, "community standards" and the law must allow it.[2]

As distributors of information, system operators face serious legal issues in the rapidly evolving on-line world. As recent cases make clear, prosecution for distributing obscene materials on-line is a reality. What are the responsibilities of sysops in handling obscene material? Are there protections? Godwin gives us some guidance:

In theory, most "hard-core" pornography qualifies as "obscenity" under the Supreme Court's test. Yet, theoretically, obscene material is commonly available in many urban areas; this perhaps signifies the relevant laws, when they do exist, are underenforced. At EFF, however, we have been telling system operators that there is no legal basis for their assuming that the laws will remain underenforced when it comes to on-line forums.

For one thing, most of this country's law enforcement organizations have only recently become aware of the extent to which such material is traded and distributed on-line. Now that they're aware of it, they recognize the potential for prosecution. In a recent case, an Oklahoma system operator was charged under state law for distributing obscene materials, based on a CD-ROM of sexual images that he had purchased through a mainstream BBS trade magazine. He was startled to find out that something he'd purchased through normal commercial channels had the potential for leading to serious criminal liability.

Still another issue, closely related to obscenity law, is whether or not an on-line system creates the risk that children will have access to adult materials. States in general have a special interest in the welfare of children, and they may choose to prohibit the exposure of children to adult materials, even when such materials are not legally obscene. (Such materials are often termed "indecent"; that is, they violate some standard of "decency," but nevertheless are constitutionally protected. If this category seems vague, that's because it is.) In *Ginsberg v. State of New York* (1968), the Supreme Court held a state statute of this sort to be constitutional.

Although there is no general standard of care for system operators who want to prevent children from having such access, it seems clear that, for a system in a state with such a statute, an operator must make a serious effort to bar minors from access to on-line adult material. (A common measure—soliciting a photocopy of a driver's license—is inadequate in my opinion. There's no reason to think a child would be unable to send in a photocopy of a parent's driver's license.)

In addition to the risk, there are some protections for system operators who are concerned about obscene materials. For example, the system operator who merely possesses, but does not distribute, obscene materials cannot constitutionally be prosecuted. In the 1969 case *Stanley v. Georgia*, the Supreme Court held that the right to possess such materials in one's own home is constitutionally protected. Thus, even if you have obscene materials on the Internet node you run out of your house, you're on safe ground as long as they're not accessible by outsiders who log onto your system.

And, in the 1959 case *Smith v. California*, the Court held that criminal obscenity statutes, like the great majority of all criminal laws, must require the government to prove "scienter" (essentially, "guilty knowledge" on the defendant's part) before that defendant can be found guilty. So, if the government can't prove beyond a reasonable doubt that a system operator knew or should have known about the obscene material on the system, the operator cannot be held liable for an obscenity crime.

In short, you can't constitutionally be convicted merely for possessing obscene material or for distributing obscene material you didn't know about.[3]

The question of whether something is obscene has reemerged as the hot topic of the digital '90s as more and more people turn to on-line services to satiate adult-oriented needs. However, the lines are clearly drawn between material that is merely obscene and material that qualifies as child pornography. Godwin explains the legal system's interpretation of child pornography:

> When the issue is child pornography, however, the rules change. Here's one of the federal child porn statutes:
>
> 18 USC 2252: Certain activities relating to material involving the sexual exploitation of minors.
>
> (a) Any person who—
>
> (1) knowingly transports or ships in interstate or foreign commerce by any means including by computer or mails, any visual depiction, if—
>
> (A) the producing of such visual depiction involves the use of a minor engaging in sexually explicit conduct; and
>
> (B) such visual depiction is of such conduct; or
>
> (2) knowingly receives, or distributes, any visual depiction that has been transported or shipped in interstate or foreign commerce by any means including by computer or mailed or knowingly reproduces any visual depiction for distribution in interstate or foreign commerce by any means including by computer or through the mails if—
>
> (A) the producing of such visual depiction involves the use of a minor engaging in sexually explicit conduct; and
>
> (B) such visual depiction is of such conduct;
>
> shall be punished as provided in subsection (b) of this section.
>
> (b) Any individual who violates this section shall be fined not more than $100,000, or imprisoned not more than 10 years, or both, but, if such individual has a prior conviction under this section, such individual shall be fined not more than $200,000, or imprisoned not less than five years nor more than 15 years, or both. Any organization which violates this section shall be fined not more than $250,000. (N.B. For the purposes of federal law, "minor" means "under age 18"; it does not refer to the age of consent in a particular state.)

This statute illustrates some of the differences between the world of obscenity law and that of child pornography law. For one thing, the statute does not address the issue of whether the material in question is "obscene." There's no issue of community standards or of "serious" artistic value. For all practical purposes, the law of child pornography is wholly separate from the law of obscenity.

Here's the reason for the separation: "obscenity" laws are aimed at forbidden expression—they assume that some things are socially harmful by virtue of being expressed or depicted. In contrast, child porn laws are not aimed at expression at all. Instead, they're designed to promote the protection of children by trying to destroy a market for materials the production of which requires the sexual use of children.

This rationale for the child pornography laws has a number of legal consequences. First, under the federal statute, material that depicts child sex, but in which a child has not been used, does not qualify as child pornography. Such material would include all textual depictions of such activity, from Nabokov's novel *Lolita* to the rankest, most offensive newsgroups on Usenet, all of which are protected by the First Amendment (assuming that, in addition to not being child pornography, they're also not obscene).

Second, the federal child-porn statute is limited to visual depictions (this is not true for all state statutes), but does not apply to all visual depictions: computer-generated or altered material that appears to be child pornography, but that did not in fact involve the sexual use of a real child, would not be punishable under the federal statute cited above. This makes sense in light of the policy if real children aren't being sexually abused, the conduct these statutes are trying to prevent has not occurred.

Although prosecutors have had little trouble up to now in proving at trial that actual children have been used to create the child porn GIF images at issue, we can anticipate that, as computer graphics tools grow increasingly powerful, a defendant will someday argue that a particular image was created by computer rather than scanned from a child porn photograph.

Third, since the laws are aimed at destroying the market for child pornography, and since the state has a very powerful interest in the safety of children, even the mere possession of child porn can be punished. (Compare: the mere possession of obscene materials is constitutionally protected.)

Fourth, the federal law, as interpreted by most federal courts, does not require that it be proved that the defendant knows that a "model" is a minor. In most jurisdictions, a defendant can be convicted for possession of child porn even if he can prove that he believed the model was an adult. If you can prove that you did not even know you possessed the image at all, you should be safe.

If your knowledge falls somewhere in between—you knew you had the image, but did not know what it depicted, or that is was sexual in its content—the law is less clear. (In other words, it's not yet clear whether it is a defense for a system administrator to claim he didn't even know he possessed the image, either because it had been uploaded by a user without his knowledge or because it had appeared in "pass-through" mail or through a Usenet newsfeed.)

In sum, then, the child porn statutes create additional problems for the system administrator who wants to avoid criminal liability and minimize the risk of a disruptive search and seizure.[4]

I've spoken to many system operators who live in fear that child porn images will be uploaded to their systems. Not all operators screen their upload content and they might unwittingly distribute child porn. Godwin describes all of the straightforward and indirect ways porn gets online:

> Although these problems pervade the world of the Internet, the easiest case to understand is the microcomputer-based BBS. The operator of a BBS typically dedicates a computer and one or more phone lines at her home or business for the use of a "virtual community" of users. Each user calls up the BBS and leaves public messages (or, in many cases, GIFs) that can be read by all other users, or private mail (which may include GIFs) that can be read by a particular user, or both. BBSs become forums—digital public houses, salons, and Hyde Park corners—for their users, and users with similar interests can associate with one another without being hindered by the accidents of geography. By some estimates, there are currently more than 40,000 BBSs throughout North America, ranging from low-end free-access BBSs with only one or two phone lines to BBSs run by companies, government agencies, user groups, and other organizations.

> A step up from the BBS in complexity is the conferencing system or information service. These systems differ in capacity from BBSs: they have the capability of serving dozens, or hundreds, of users at the same time. But they're like BBSs in that uploaded files can be found at a fixed geographic location. A further step up are entities like Fidonet and Usenet, which, because they're highly distributed, decentralized conferencing systems, add complications to the legal issues raised by the computerization of sexual images.

> Internet nodes and the systems that connect to them, for example, may carry such images unwittingly, either through unencoded mail or through uninspected Usenet newsgroups. The store-and-forward nature of message distribution on these systems means that such traffic may exist on a system at some point in time, even though it did not originate there and even though it won't ultimately end up there. What's more, even if a sysadmin refuses to carry the distributed forms that are most likely to carry graphic images, she may discover that sexually graphic images have been distributed through a newsgroup that is not obviously sexually oriented.

> Depending on the type of system he or she runs, a system operator may not know (and may not be able to know) much about the system's GIF-file traffic, especially if his or her system allows GIFs to be traded in private mail. Other operators may devote all or part of their systems to adult-oriented content, including image files.

> Regardless of how their systems are run, operators often create risks for themselves under the mistaken assumption that since this kind of material is commonplace, it must be legal, and even if it's illegal, they can't be

prosecuted for something they don't know about. EFF's Legal Services Department has been working actively to educate system operators about the risks of making these assumptions.[5]

If history is any guide, the Internet will not indefinitely remain the unrestricted communications medium it currently is. Just like the FCC (Federal Communications Commission) patrols the radio waves, and rating systems differentiate X-rated adult films from G-rated general family fare, the Internet will eventually see its own regulatory agency come into being. Pedophiles circulating child pornography images on the Internet are being arrested. Bulletin boards are being prosecuted for offenses illegal, not on their home turf, but in distant states. Universities are blocking access to adult-oriented Usenet newsgroups. The wagons are circling, and the lines are being drawn. The overwhelming majority of the active Internet population vehemently disdains the notion of any kind of digital restriction whatsoever. However, if a governing body is brought into place to establish general, internationally accepted laws, hopefully the Internet population will establish themselves as the vocal and knowledgeable authorities that they are, and not leave the policy-making to off-line amateurs.

Notes

[1] James Anthony Froude, "Calvinism." In *Short Studies on Great Subjects.* New York: C. Scribner & Sons, n.d.

[2-5] All citations are taken from the article by Mike Godwin, "Sex and the Single Sysadmin." *Internet World* (April 1994).

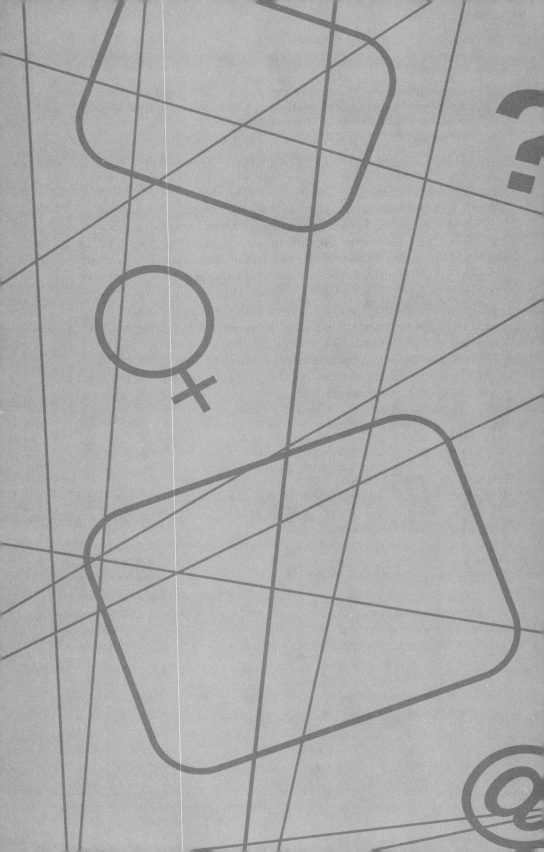

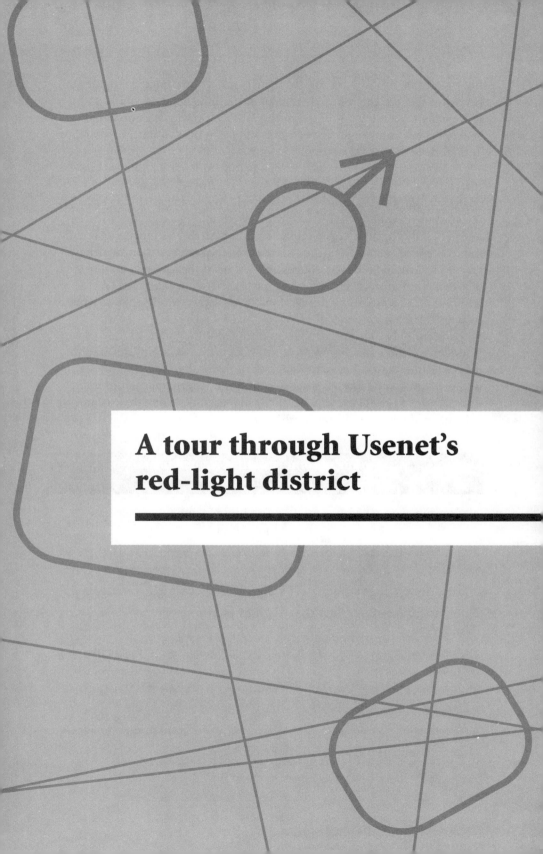

A tour through Usenet's red-light district

Love—and its illegitimate stepchild, lust—have found a nonjudgmental home on Usenet. Currently there are approximately 200 sexually and romantically driven Usenet newsgroups, where millions of people daily exchange ideas, find romantic partners, and learn more about mainstream and esoteric areas of sexuality.

In this chapter we'll take an inside look at what is discussed in many of the adult-oriented newsgroups. In terms of influence and "name recognition," alt.sex is widely considered the virtual kingpin of the sexually driven Usenet newsgroups. With over 440,000 loyal readers, it is generally the first stop on people's cybersexual Net journey. According to the news.lists newsgroup, alt.sex is the fourth most popular newsgroup of thousands offered. Interestingly, four of the top ten newsgroups are sexual in nature, including alt.sex.stories (over 500,000 readers), alt.binaries.pictures.erotica (over 450,000 devotees), and rec.arts.erotica (over 370,000 fans).

Seemingly every aspect of sexuality, from the bland to the bizarre, is fodder for the Usenet newsgroups. There are newsgroups devoted to diaper fetishes, latex lovers, bondage aficionados, bestiality, scatology, as well as groups aimed at teaching shy computer types the rules of dating in the '90s. So buckle up your seatbelt, sit back, and enjoy this risqué ride down the information superhighway.

A sampling of some sexually oriented forums currently on Usenet	
alt.amazon-women.admirers	Worshiping women you have to look up to
alt.binaries.pictures.erotica.-bestiality	Pictures of sex with animals
alt.binaries.pictures.erotica	Gigabytes of copyright violations
alt.binaries.pictures.erotica-.bondage	BDSM pictures
alt.binaries.pictures.erotica-.blondes	Copyright violations featuring blondes
alt.binaries.pictures.erotica-.cartoons	Copyright violations featuring toons
alt.binaries.pictures.erotica.d	Discussing erotic copyright violations
alt.binaries.pictures.erotica.fetish	Fetish pictures

A sampling of some sexually oriented forums currently on Usenet (Continued)

alt.binaries.pictures.erotica.female	Copyright violations featuring females
alt.binaries.pictures.erotica.furry	Erotic furry images
alt.binaries.pictures.erotica.male	Copyright violations featuring males
alt.binaries.pictures.erotica.orientals	Copyright violations featuring Asians
alt.binaries.pictures.girlfriends	Pictures of the SO
alt.binaries.pictures.supermodels	Yet more copyright violations
alt.binaries.pictures.tasteless	Eccchhh, that last one was *sick*!
alt.binaries.pictures.utilities	Posting of pictures-related utilties
alt.binaries.sounds.erotica	Download moans and groans here
alt.clothing.lingerie	Celebration of the undergarment
alt.christnet.sex	Some of them still do that you know
alt.dead.porn.stars	…and the diseases that killed them, next on Geraldo
alt.hi.are.you.cute	Are there a lot of pathetic people on the net or what?
alt.homosexual	Same as alt.sex.homosexual
alt.irc	Internet Relay Chat material
alt.irc.ircii	IRC, the sequel
alt.irc.announce	Announcements about IRC (Moderated)
alt.irc.hottub	Discussion of the IRC channel #hottub
alt.irc.questions	How-to questions about IRC
alt.irc.undernet	Discussions about the undernet
alt.lycra	The WunderFabrik
alt.mag.playboy	Four decades of appreciation or degradation—your pick
alt.magazines.pornographic	Like alt.sex.magazines, only different

A sampling of some sexually oriented forums currently on Usenet (Continued)

alt.magick.sex	Pursuing spirituality through sexuality and vice versa
alt.pantyhose	Stockings are sexier
alt.party	Parties, celebration and general debauchery
alt.personals	Do you really want to meet someone this way?
alt.personals.ads	Geek seeks dweeb. Object: low-level interfacing
alt.personals.bi	Personals by or seeking bisexuals
alt.personals.big-folks	Romance for large people
alt.personals.bondage	Are you tied up this evening?
alt.personals.fat	Romance for fat people
alt.personals.fetish	Romance for object-oriented people
alt.personals.misc	Dweeb seeks geek. Object: low-level interfacing
alt.personals.poly	Hi there, do you multiprocess?
alt.personals.spanking	Oedipus gave this room a thumbs up
alt.personals.spanking-.punishment	In search of a bad butt burn
alt.politics.homosexuality	As the name implies
alt.politics.sex	Not a good idea to mix them, sez Marilyn & Profumo
alt.polyamory	For those who maintain multiple love relationships
alt.pub.coffeehouse.amethyst	Realistic place to meet and and chat with friends
alt.pub.dragons-inn	Fantasy virtual reality pub similar to alt.callahans
alt.pub.havens-rest	Fantasy virtual reality pub similar to alt.callahans

A sampling of some sexually oriented forums currently on Usenet (Continued)

alt.recovery.addiction.sexual	Recovering sex addicts
alt.romance	Discussion about the romantic side of love
alt.romance.chat	Talk about no sex
alt.romance.unhappy	alt.angst on the run
alt.sex	Postings of a prurient nature
alt.sex.anal	Sexual acts involving the anus
alt.sex.bears	Hairy homosexual men
alt.sex.bestiality	Happiness is a warm puppy
alt.sex.bestiality.barney	For people with big, purple newt fetishes
alt.sex.bondage	Tie me, whip me, make me read the Net!
alt.sex.breast	Discussions about female breasts—big and small
alt.sex.cthulhu	It's amazing what tentacles can do
alt.sex.enemas	Cleansing the bowels is an erotic act
alt.sex.erotica.marketplace	The business of sex
alt.sex.exhibitionism	So you want to be a star
alt.sex.fat	Rollin' with the roly-poly
alt.sex.femdom	Discussions about female dominant relationships
alt.sex.fetish.amputee	Sexual attraction to missing body parts
alt.sex.fetish.diapers	They're dry and secure all day too
alt.sex.fetish.fashion	Rubber, leather, chains, and other fetish clothing
alt.sex.fetish.fa	Same as alt.sex.fat
alt.sex.fetish.feet	Kiss them. Now!
alt.sex.fetish.hair	Hair, hair, everywhere (palms even)

A sampling of some sexually oriented forums currently on Usenet (Continued)

alt.sex.fetish.orientals	The mysteries of Asia are a potent lure
alt.sex.fetish.robots	This is for you robot types
alt.sex.fetish.sportswear	For those with a fetish for sportswear
alt.sex.fetish.startrek	Illogical yet fascinating Star Trek lust
alt.sex.fetish.tickling	Laughter is the best foreplay
alt.sex.fetish.watersports	They don't mean hottub polo
alt.sex.fetish.wrestling	You'll never look at wrestling on TV the same way again
alt.sex.first-time	What was your first time like?
alt.sex.girl.watchers	Like alt.sex.voyeurism, only different
alt.sex.guns	Fuel for the pornography-incites-violence debate
alt.sex.homosexual	Homosexual relations
alt.sex.intergen	Robbing the cradle and the grave
alt.flame.cycle-sluts	Women on bikes. Don't pickup litter, pick up me.
alt.sex.magazines	Discussions of magazines with sticky pages
alt.sex.masturbation	Where one's SO is oneself
alt.sex.motss	Jesse Helms would not subscribe to this group
alt.sex.movies	Discussing the ins and outs of certain movies
alt.sex.nasal-hair	The dearth of posts must signify that nasal hair isn't sexy
alt.sex.necrophilia	Dead people as stimulus
alt.sex.nfs	Desperately needed group to discuss the pleasures and complications of remote mounting
alt.sex.NOT	Abstinence by choice or circumstance

A sampling of some sexually oriented forums currently on Usenet (Continued)

alt.sex.pedophilia	Discussing the issues around attraction to children
alt.sex.pictures	Gigabytes of copyright violations
alt.sex.pictures.female	Copyright violations featuring mostly females
alt.sex.plushies	Plush sex: Strategically Placed Holes
alt.sex.sounds	Noises from the heat of passion
alt.sex.services	The oldest profession
alt.sex.sm.fig	Sadism and masochism with mulberries
alt.sex.alt.syntax.tactical	Premise anyone?
alt.sex.spanking	Bondage for beginners
alt.sex.stories	For those who need it NOW
alt.sex.stories.d	For those who talk about needing it NOW
alt.sex.strip-clubs	Discussion of strip clubs, exotic dancers, etc.
alt.sex.telephone	Discussion of phone sex services
alt.sex.voyeurism	A lot of lurkers in this group
alt.sex.wanted	Requests for erotica, either literary or in the flesh
alt.sex.watersports	Fun in the shower
alt.sex.wizards	Questions for only true sex wizards
alt.sex.woody-allen	For the young women on the Net
alt.sexual.abuse.recovery	Helping others deal with traumatic experiences
alt.sex.zoophilia	Having sex with animals and respecting them too
alt.sex.telephone	Phone sex anyone?
alt.society.underwear	What's the big deal anyway?

**A sampling of some sexually oriented forums
currently on Usenet (Continued)**

alt.supermodels	Discussing famous and beautiful models
alt.transgendered	For transvestites and cross-dressers
alt.wedding	Till death or our lawyers do us part
clari.news.crime.sex	Sex crimes, child pornography
clari.news.sex	Sexual issues, sex-related political stories
rec.arts.bodyart	Body piercing, tattooing, etc.
rec.arts.erotica	Erotic fiction and verse (moderated)
rec.arts.pictures.erotica	Erotic pictures
rec.nude	Hobbyists interested in naturist/ nudist activities
soc.men	Issues related to men, their problems and relationships
soc.misc	Socially-oriented topics not in other groups
soc.motss	Issues pertaining to homosexuality
soc.penpals	In search of Net friendships
soc.singles	Newsgroup for single people, their activities
soc.support.transgendered	Support group for TV/TS/CDs
soc.women	Issues related to women, their problems and relationships

alt.sex and Beyond: The Usenet Sex Forums

Everything you ever wanted to know about sex, and always wanted to ask, is posted on alt.sex. If you want to know what the recovery time is after ejaculation, it's in there. If you want to know the definition of *le petit mort*, it's in there. Or if you just want to confess your longing for sheep, you'll find a place for that there, too. Every Usenet newsgroup has a defining tone of its own, and the tone of alt.sex is one where people are exploring the mechanics and dynamics of sex. To paraphrase the words of one eager poster, "I know where everything goes; I just need to know the best way to insert it."

Although people of all ages frequent alt.sex, the majority of people who post are in college, logging in from their University-sponsored accounts. At times, alt.sex feels like a never-ending dormitory party, complete with overflowing beer mugs and horny men. Although date rape cannot take place in cyberspace, one does witness a high volume of male domination and female alienation on alt.sex. A Dartmouth woman, "Beth," posted a response on the ideal penis size. The next morning, her e-mail in box was overflowing with more than 100 letters from amorous men. "It was intimidating," states Beth. "I felt like I was posting in anonymity, and suddenly I realized that hundreds of thousands of people had read my words. I didn't say I was looking for a man. I was just posting a response to a man who was worried he was too small. I was trying to make him realize that size was not as important as he believed. Next thing you know, I'm being endlessly propositioned by e-mail. I don't think I'll post again."

alt.sex is a place where folks trade secrets, confess failings or perceived failings, seek advice, or just go for the big shock-value statements. Sometimes the conversation can get quite heady, as evidenced in a long "clitoral vs. vaginal orgasm" thread (exchange). "Bec-Bec's" belief that a "woman's vaginal orgasm is basically comparable to the contraction of the anus" elicited a flood of rebuttals. "CJMFreud," who has taught Human Sexuality at the university level for several years, posted that "according to Masters & Johnson's decades of research, there is no physiological or psychological difference between vaginal and clitoral orgasms. In fact, vaginal orgasms happen due to the rubbing of the clitoral hood on the clitoris during penetration. So all orgasms are clitoral." After about a dozen posts all from men, "Debby" piped up, "It always amuses me to see men discuss female orgasms like they are the ultimate authority!"

However, beyond the college-age antics is a wealth of information. As you read through the thousands of posts, a pattern becomes clear. If a sexual fallacy is posted, it will soon be debunked. Beyond the hormonally charged males who troll through this newsgroup looking for dates, or the chance to flame unsuspecting souls, lies a wealth of sexually sophisticated people who are eager to share their knowledge. alt.sex should be a newbie's first stop on the well-traveled, erotically driven sidestreets of Usenet.

The FAQ for alt.sex is impressive in its scope of accurate and timely information, from AIDS prevention tips and treatment to the mechanics of giving a "hand job." To receive a copy of this comprehensive FAQ, look for it in alt.sex, news.answers, or alt.answers. If you can't find it there, you can find the latest version via ftp at rtfm.mit.edu in /pub/usenet/alt-sex. As a last resort, contact the FAQ editors, David Johnson and "Snugglebunny," at superdj@cs.mcgill.ca. Below is an excerpt of an alt.sex FAQ.

Reprint of part of the February 1994 alt.sex FAQ

TABLE OF CONTENTS:

Category 1. Alt.sex terms and acronyms

Category 2. Where can I find...?
c2-1 Where can I find this FAQ?
c2-2 What versions of the purity test are there?
c2-3 Where can I get the purity tests?
c2-4 Where can I find alt.sex stories? are there archive sites for them?
c2-5 Where can I find binary pictures and/or movies?
c2-6 What are good books to read up on?
c2-7 What stores sell sex-toys, etc.?
c2-8 Where can I find the archives for alt.sex.bondage & alt.sex.stories?
c2-9 Where can I find the Index to USENET Erotica?
c2-1Ø Where can I order from via catalog?
c2-11 Where can I find sex-related mailing lists?
c2-12 Where can I find additional sex topics on USENET?

Category 3. Practical and "how-to" stuff
c3-1 What should I do to make (the first attempt at) vaginal sex easiest?
c3-2 What should I do to make (the first attempt at) oral sex easiest?
c3-3 What should I do to make (the first attempt at) anal sex easiest?
c3-4 How does one give a hand job?
c3-5 What is the Venus butterfly?
c3-6 What is and where is the G-spot?
c3-7 How can females ejaculate?
c3-8 What about oral/vaginal sex during a woman's period?
c3-9 What can one do about premature ejaculation?
c3-1Ø What are some good positions to try out?

Category 4. Biological stuff
c4-1 What are the contents of semen?
c4-2 How much semen and how many sperm are in a single ejaculate?
c4-3 Does what I eat affect the taste of semen/vaginal fluids?
c4-4 What's the average length and width penis?
c4-5 What's the average depth vagina?
c4-6 What are blue balls?

Reprint of part of the February 1994 alt.sex FAQ (Continued)

c4-7 Is Spanish fly dangerous?
c4-8 Is it possible to get pregnant from anal sex?

Category 5. Sexual aids
c5-1 Should I buy a vibrator?
  What kind of vibrators are there?
  Do vibrators 'desensitize' women?
  Can I be replaced by a vibrator?
c5-2 What is a good lubricant to use? (future addition)

Category 6. General stuff
c6-1 What is circumcision and why is it done?
c6-2 What percentage of men and women masturbate? and at what frequency?
c6-3 How are the bases defined again? (i.e. 1st base = kissing, etc.)
c6-4 What is the M-spot?
c6-5 How to shave your pubic region (female)

Category 7. STDs
c7-1 How is the AIDS virus transmitted? and what does a HIV test show?
c7-2 What is HPV (human papilloma virus)? treatment?
c7-3 The major sexually transmitted disease (STDs) and their symptoms (Gonorrhea, Syphilis, Genital Herpes, AIDS,
  Pubic Lice (Crabs), Nonspecific Urethritis (NSU), Hepatitis B are covered)
c7-4 What are venereal warts? treatment?

Category 8. Contraception
c8-1 What are the various methods of contraception? and their effectiveness rates? and their associated risks
  if any?
c8-2 What kinds of condoms are there?
c8-3 Is the Pill safe? (future addition)
c8-4 What about Norplant? (future addition)

Category 9. Myths

Appendix 1. List of contributors

Reprinted courtesy of David Johnson.

This list represents a few of the thousands of posts found in alt.sex the week of July 10, 1994.

1 Erections (3 msgs)

2 Penis size - organizations (2 msgs)

3 Who is the best looking TV anchor woman?

4 First Time Masturbating (3 msgs)

5 Penis with a mind of its own ! (4 msgs)

6 I'M SO UNHAPPY(and could use some cheering up) (16 msgs)

7 Question about Strip Bars (5 msgs)

8 Beware of Roman Catholic Corruption (9 msgs)

9 What do women see in men anyway? (53 msgs)

1Ø Clitoral vs. Vaginal Orgasm (12 msgs)

11 Fuck (2 msgs)

12 Hitachi Magic Wand (2 msgs)

13 Jill Shaller scratches cat butt. (2 msgs)

14 Jill/Stacy thing

15 blow up doll breasts

16 do women have rape fantasies? (15 msgs)

17 Best looking woman anchor (3 msgs)

18 Telling children (19 msgs)

19 Lust for Madonna (6 msgs)

2Ø Ejaculation recovery time? (8 msgs)

21 P-ing in the shower.

22 Threesome

23 purity

24 SURVEY FOR MEN ONLY (7 msgs)

25 Smoking (2 msgs)

26 Adult GIF mailing List... (4 msgs)

27 I NEED HELP JERKING OFF (4 msgs)

28 Females and Felatio (3Ø msgs)

29 ALT.SEX.FANTASIES (2 msgs)

3Ø Le Petit Mort (what is?) (4 msgs)

31 Sex with animals (2 msgs)

32 Wanted:Slang terms for masturbation (13 msgs)

33 INCEST (5 msgs)

34 lesbians look (3 msgs)

35 Morality (4 msgs)

36 Vitamins and fluorescent yellow urine... (5 msgs)

37 P--ing in the sink

38 Are there any women in this newsgroup? (19 msgs)

39 REQUEST: Purity Tests? (2 msgs)

4Ø TRUE Origin of the word FUCK

41 What is the average penile girth? (7 msgs)

42 Breasts Stimulation (2 msgs)

43 FIRST TIME MASTURBATING (3 msgs)

44 good x rated video (3 msgs)

~

alt.sex.bondage   "Master Charles," system operator (sysop) of the largest Dominance/submission (D/s) bulletin board on the East Coast, refers
to alt.sex.bondage (a.s.b) as "brutal." If a well-respected "Dom" finds
alt.sex.bondage a tough crowd, you can imagine how it can affect the ordinary vanilla person who is eager to add some new flavors to his or her
repertoire.

A newbie with the nerve to post in alt.sex.bondage, without taking
the time to lurk (read, not post) for several weeks, can expect to be flamed
to blackened perfection. One young woman, a professional writer by
trade, and new to the world of D/s, wrote a thoughtful, expansive post on
her love for her new Master. The experiences she was relating were typical
of a submissive, but since they were all new to her, she was in the shout-
ing-her-devoted-love-from-the-rafters phase. Within hours, her love-
filled post of adoration was savaged by some regulars from the
alt.sex.bondage crowd. Her worship-laden post was discounted by many
as the insubstantial ramblings of an inconsequential newbie.

According to the official monthly welcome, written by "Big Al,"
alt.sex.bondage "serves as something of a catchall group for all of the
Bondage & Discipline, Dominance and Submission, Sadism & Masoch-
ism (BDSM) spectrum. You can find technical advice, jokes, relationship
and morality arguments, fiction, and almost anything else you want pre-
sented in a BDSM-positive light." According to the welcome post, "Over
180,000 people read a.s.b., but only about 1 to 200 people actually post
with any degree of regularity. The vast majority of people just lurk."

~

alt.sex.wanted   alt.sex.wanted is brutal in its lusty honesty. No one is
purporting to talk about sexual issues, ideologies, fashions, or fetishes.
The theme and purpose of this newsgroup is as pure as the "undriven"
snow: getting laid. According to this newsgroup's FAQ, a typical clueless
newbie who stumbles upon this newsgroup usually says something like
"Hey, Dudes! I just stumbled onto this group—is it really for what it
seems like? I only saw one post from a girl saying she was desperate
to get laid, but I didn't know how to respond. I posted an ad saying I
wuz horny six times, but I haven't heard anything yet, except a follow-up telling me to read the FAQ. There don't seem to be any women!
I WANNA GET LAID!! My spouse is a dud, and I need some action;
call me at 555-BOZO."

According to alt.sex.wanted's moderator, Ed Ming, the "group was created to get the requests for erotic stories out of alt.sex.stories (at which it has failed). It *does* serve to get the I WANNA GET LAID, DUDES! posts off of most the rest of the Net, and thus justifies its existence. In short, alt.sex.wanted is for requesting explicit GIF sites, literary erotica, exchanges of erotic e-mail, and yes, trying to set up physical carnal encounters. This doesn't mean you *will* actually get what you want, just that you can try. It also has been used for some time to post ads for erotic BBSs, Party Lines, etc., since there really wasn't any place else more appropriate."

Ming adds: "Saying what gender and what your sexual orientation are will keep you and other people from being annoyed by time-wasting, confused e-mail. If you don't say what *you* are, as well as what/who you are looking for, how will you connect? The usual convention has a set of acronyms: ISO for 'In Search Of,' SWM for 'Straight White Male,' GBF for 'Gay Black Female,' BiAF for 'Bisexual Asian Female,' and so forth. Usually on alt.sex.wanted the 'S' at the beginning stands for Straight, and not for Single, although this isn't a hard and fast rule."

In response to an inquiry about a post "from a girl saying she was desperate to get laid," Ming advises that "such is *probably* (but not certainly) a fake. News articles are occasionally forged; passwords are stolen or foolishly shared; people forget to log out. A fair number of the ads posted are fakes; perhaps not especially from females, but they seem to be subject to the most enthusiastic, misguided responses. If it seems too good to be true, remember it might not be true. Be polite at first, and make sure it's real. ESPECIALLY, do not believe anyone who gives an e-mail address other than the one in the header. Anyone who says, 'Please send e-mail to my friend biff@foo.bar.baz.net' is almost certainly NOT a friend of that person. For that matter, don't believe 'I'm using a friend's account, but please respond to mine at grep@mung.blot.net' too readily, either. Ladies and wenches, do not be surprised if doubts are expressed when you first post. It will pass soon, if you persist."

When a woman does post in alt.sex.wanted, she is bound to unwittingly become the belle of the digital ball. "Jessica" stated that her simple post received 21 responses. "Ten were complete 'wannafucks' and the rest either comments or requests of a more rational nature. Sometimes I wonder if these guys have too much time on their hands."

However, few women post "sex-wanted" declarations here. When one is found, it is generally from a "professional" gal interested in supplementing her portfolio, such as the one found from "Monique." "I'm very bi, love talking about sex, and love to dominate men. I love to make videos of myself and have guys masturbate over me. I'm 36C-25-35 with short black hair and blue eyes. If you want the video, send $25."

Do real, live women actually read alt.sex.wanted? According to Ming, "They do. Some even post somewhat regularly. Some just lurk. In my non-random sampling I noticed about a dozen or so females posting. They mainly seem scarce because there are so many guys. This reflects the Net. (The median estimate is around 1 in 6 a.s.w readers is female.) Also, when a female shows up, clueless folks tend to e-mail 'wannafuck' messages no matter *what* she has said. This means many of them don't post, only listen. The law of supply and demand is on their side; they don't have to step forward publicly."

If there is a singular tone on alt.sex.wanted, it is despair, and is best summed up by "Karl's" post: "I previously posted a 'SWM ISO SF (single white male in search of single female)' on this group and got zero replies to my post. The only two reasons I can come up with are that either there are no women reading this group, or I'm a pathetic loser and no one wants me."

Digital humanity cries out to get lucky in alt.sex.wanted

585 messages have been posted in the last 14 days
[585 messages in 367 discussion threads]

1 SWM seeks Hispanic or Asian female for 'fun' in Chicago (3 msgs)
2 SWM seeks Sexy Latin and Oriental females in Chicago for 'fun'
3 Texas GWM
4 NYC girl needs a girl for sex and fun
5 va females wanted (2 msgs)
6 Hi!.... (2 msgs)
7 SWF 25 (hetero) wants to try erotic e-mail (3 msgs)
8 Looking
9 M=E=L=B=O=U=R=N=E : I will keep lookin' for LUV !!! (3 msgs)
1Ø SEX AND SOCIAL BULLETINS FROM THE FRONT LINES (3 msgs)
11 Are There any Horny ladies in Ft.laud. Please rea
12 PROSPECTS
13 RE HOT TO HEAR FROM YOU
14 Young Male Looking For Same - Memphis, TN
15 1st CLASS US MALE (2 msgs)
16 SWF's in Manhatten
17 Are there any women in this newsgroup? (16 msgs)
18 King iso Queen in CA
19 Mark E. Dassad
2Ø Request from 27 y/o DWM
21 Survey: Car Sex (8 msgs)

~

alt.sex.bestiality   A dog can be a man's lover as well as his best friend in alt.sex.bestiality. Experiences relayed on this forum have nothing to do with taking the kids to the San Diego Zoo, and everything to do with exploring intimate physical relationships with a wide spectrum of four-legged beasts, from dogs to horses and assorted other farm animals.

There are plenty of taboo photos available for downloading on alt.sex.bestiality, from relatively tame photos of a lion's erect penis to action shots of a man having sexual intercourse with a calf, to a woman performing fellatio on a dog. A majority of the posts feature bestiality erotica, "tales" both fictional and true-life, of men and women's sexual dalliances with animals. "Matt" posts a zoo fantasy about Amanda and Victor-the-dog. The story goes along the lines of "Amanda wondered if Victor remembered almost having sex with her in the garage. She did notice that the dog's penis no longer expanded out of its sheath when he saw Amanda. She wondered if she would have to seduce the dog now that they were finally going to be alone, and how hard this would be."

"Anna," a mother of two and a self-professed canine sex lover who engages in animal sex while her husband looks on, provides a lengthy dissertation and guide to canine sex. She posts: "Zoofili, sexual intercourse with animals, has for a long time been a forbidden subject, considered 'sick,' unethical, and 'kinky.' I would like to illuminate my knowledge of canine sex, to share my insights with other women who have a similar interest…. In this guide I will cover cunnilingus, vaginal sex, and fellatio. Anal sex can be performed, but I find that you have to be very experienced with anal sex to make love to a dog in that manner, so I've chosen not to include that area."

Many people who frequent alt.sex.bestiality are seeking to find like-minded animal-lusting aficionados. "Rob" posts that he'd like to meet "another zoo live on IRC (Internet Relay Chat) to get something going." A West Coast biker grouses about his problem finding "sexually intact dogs," and his experience with the classifieds. His ad, rejected by several newspapers, but accepted by one Bay Area journal read, "Kinky, bearded biker boy is turned on by big, horny dogs. Wrestling, licking, sniffing, and more. If you've got one, call, and watch or join in on the fun."

However, along with the self-acceptance of "loving zoos, taking good care of their pets" are a sprinkling of negative posts from non-zoos. "Iggy" posts: "Why don't you name this new group, alt.sex.animals.rape? Because that's what you are really doing!" However, a non-zoo posting in a zoo-friendly environment is bound to get more flames than fans, as judged by the responses, such as the one from "Elf" who replied: "Why don't you go find a newsgroup dedicated to gambling and call it alt.race-horses.run.till.you.die or visit rec.arts.cooking and tell them to rename it rec.arts.eating.dead.animals." Or "Iggy" who posted, "Once again someone has shown their profound ignorance of the facts. Personally when a male dog mounts me, if anything rape would be the other way around, and you can't really rape the willing, so…."

The zoophile humor found on alt.sex.bestiality really can't be found anywhere else. "Matt" posts that he had "played" with his black lab. Two hours after fellatio, he had a dentist appointment. "Matt" found himself "lying in the chair, mouth open, with a hygienist staring down" his throat. Then it hit him. Were there still any hairs left in his mouth? What if there was one caught between his teeth? The image of the hygienist encountering the dog hairs embedded in his throat struck him so hard that he nearly laughed.

The modus operandi of the alt.sex.bestiality reader can best be summed up as found in "Shadow Walker's" digital signature (a signature file is a motto and/or ascii artwork that follows every post, and that is created by the poster), which reads: "To walk among the shadows of society. Forever an outcast, is that what it means to be a zoophile? If it means, I can be with a loved one, then I proudly say 'I am a zoophile.'"

∼

alt.sex.bestiality.barney   "Why does this newsgroup exist?" I posted in alt.sex.bestiality.barney. "Why not?" answered Ennio Phillips. There is little rhyme or reason to alt.sex.bestiality.barney except an underlying disdain, paired with outpourings of affection, for the purple dinosaur.

The posting volume is light, with about 20 or so messages posted in a 14-day period on average. Every aspect of Barney is discussed and appraised. "Has anyone else ever noticed that Barney doesn't have any genitals?" posted "Ken." The occasional psychotic post rears its ugly prehistoric head here as well, such as the one from "Will." "If you really think about it, Barney is just an imaginary stuffed purple dinosaur. It would be a waste of time planning to kill him. Why not do something really cool, and kill a person instead?" "Lentilboy" attempts to set him straight, "We do not want to kill Barney, we want to have sex with him (it). Why do so many people make the false assumption that we hate Barney and want to kill him?" "Because we do," posts a chorus from the kill-Barney faction.

A post found in alt.sex.bestiality.barney

Subject: Barney = Satan
Subj: Barney = Satan

Barney, the cute purple dinosaur, is Satan.

Proof:

Given: Barney is a cute purple dinosaur.

Extract the Roman numerals:
(and remember that the Romans had no letter 'U',
they used 'V' instead)

CVTE PVRPLE DINOSAVR
CV V L DI V

Add them:
$1\varnothing\varnothing + 5 + 5 + 5\varnothing + 5\varnothing\varnothing + 1 + 5 = 666$
Q. E. D. We suspected it all along.

∽

alt.sex.services   If you're looking for the best "bang" your buck can buy in Las Vegas, need to know the phone number of a Boston area dominatrix, or the inside skinny on adult phone services, alt.sex.services is your harlotry referral service in cyberspace. Very few women post on this newsgroup. In fact, most of the females posting appear to be digital streetwalkers.

One woman is "interested in providing a service of administering enemas to willing individuals on a cash basis while wearing standard nurse, rubber, leather, or maid outfits, without any sexual contact." "Chezamor Escorts" posts an ad stating that they are the service for "men seeking a male companion." "Mistress Victoria," including a phone number, sends a message directed to "Minneapolis submissives" who are "interested in all aspects of B&D, erotic body worship, and the feminization of males."

A majority of the posts consist of true-life experiences from the massage parlor and streetwalker fronts. Men inquire about which establishments offer more than a mere massage, how much the extra pleasures cost, what street corners in each city offer the prettiest, most accommodating women, and on and on. And most of the men who post make use of anonymous mail servers. One such man, "Jeff," posted his experience with both streetwalkers and massage parlors in Austin, Texas, and San Francisco, California. He opened his review with an editorial about looks versus sexual performance. "I've noticed a very strong correlation between how pretty a woman looks and how bad the sex is. It seems like almost all of the pretty women I pick up are in a hurry to finish, and not willing to do anything extra. However, many of the average women I pick up are much more into it and seem to be actually enjoying the encounter."

"Wayne's" post about prostitution in St. Louis resulted in advice from "Leonard," stating there is "nothing worthwhile in St. Louis proper, unless you want to play STD (sexually transmitted disease) roulette with a scuzzy-looking streetwalker or find yourself visiting the lavish accommodations provided by St. Louis's finest to unsuspecting johns."

A man who indulged his fantasy to be dominated by a woman filled in the newsgroup about his experience. "She was wearing a black bra and panties, garter belt with stockings, and stiletto heels. I was instructed to kiss her legs, from one toe to another…. Time sure flew by, before I knew it, I was laying flat on my back, with my wrists chained to my ankles. She sat on me stroking my…." He closes his post with some tips "to remember when looking for a mistress. Make sure to hire someone who will respect your bounds. Remember that there will probably be no sex involved beyond a hand job. Make sure that all toys are sterilized before use, and be sure to talk first on the phone and in person. If you don't feel comfortable, you can always leave."

It would be interesting to read the point of view of the prostitutes/madams/dominatrices, and so on in this newsgroup. Unfortunately, those viewpoints appear not to be represented in alt.sex.services. However, if you're a traveling salesman who craves to know the ins-and-outs of the hottest joints in town, alt.sex.services is a virtual encyclopedic reference source on everyone's favorite deadly sin.

⁓

alt.sex.fat   In a society where some consider waifish fashion model Kate Moss's angular figure perfection, it is refreshing to find an environment—albeit a digital one—where heavyset people revel in their body size and actively discourage feelings of unworthiness. According to "Michael," a regular poster, "alt.sex.fat is a great place to discuss any sort of sex that involves one or more fat people. You can probably get away with talking about other non-sex stuff too that relates to fat people. In fact, just about the only thing you really can't get away with is talking about dieting."

This newsgroup is filled with lively discussions about attracting FA (fat admirer) mates, announcing local NAAFA (National Association to Aid Fat Americans) meetings, and exchanging erotica of all kinds, from videos featuring fleshy performers to steamy text featuring corpulent characters.

Fat admiration (FA as they refer to it in alt.sex.fat) has been released from its dark, gloomy closet on alt.sex.fat and proudly revels in its gargantuan glory. One BBW (big, beautiful woman) confessed that she has "always wanted to be fatter" and now "weighs 300 pounds (up from 140)." She wants nothing more than to "get fatter, at least 500 pounds" because she finds fleshiness "the most wonderful, pleasing, erotic" experience. "MadScout" posts that he is 530 pounds and "loves being fat" and seeks to "gain even more weight."

Others harbor flesh-enhancing fantasies, the notion of purposely overfeeding a partner to create a fat, fantasy figure. "Eric" wonders why being a "feeder" is "frowned upon" on alt.sex.fat. "Hans" answers that "control with complete disregard for the consequences beyond satiation is dangerous and harmful. And it is all about control. Why else would one go to the trouble of fattening someone up when there are plenty of large men and women who are eagerly searching for a partner?"

In response to a woman's complaint about the dearth of FA men, "HeatherNY" replies that "being large should have nothing to do with finding sexual partners." Heather, a bubbly and beautiful 270-pound woman who frequently appears on mainstream talk shows proselytizing the virtues of girth, posts that she "has no problem getting dates." She credits "confidence" in her "mind, ambition, and fat body…. Start smiling at the gorgeous men in the stores that you think would never give you a look. You will be surprised at the results." "Jillian" resents "Heather's" upbeat attitude, rebutting, "I don't need you as a pom-pom waving cheerleader. I like myself just fine, thank you. I have zillions of wonderful qualities, and think I'm cute, but I don't date either."

"Michael" posts: "I wish I could find a woman who thinks fat guys are sexy because we could have a lot of fun together. There's a warm heart beating in the center of me, but women can't seem to see past the outside of me." "Nikidee" aligns her beliefs with Heather's. "I don't think I'm an optimist, but a realist. I think we all have the chance to find someone to be with, regardless of our size. Maybe it will take longer, but if we don't live with hope, then the work truly is bleak. I kind of feel like it's like being in a middle of a storm…and there are dark clouds and rain surrounding you, but in your mind and heart you know that there might be a rainbow. And the hope to see a rainbow is enough to get you through the storm."

"Suzanne" concludes that "there are willing partners out there. However, as fat people we may be conditioned not to expect willing sexual partners. After all, hasn't society told us we are undesirable and unattractive? Who would be looking for partners when all someone has experienced is rejection? Every one of us deserves to have a healthy, fulfilling sexual life. We are not ugly, we are not undesirable, and we are not sexual misfits." The posts of alt.sex.fat reveal predominately caring, compassionate, and helpful people who are eager to break ill-conceived, malicious, societal stereotypes and inspire less-confident members to hold their heads high and live their lives to the fullest. Another worthy Usenet newsgroup that provides valuable support for larger folks is alt.support.big-folks.

∿

alt.sex.femdom   alt.sex.femdom was formed in February 1994 as an offshoot of alt.sex.bondage. According to the group's biweekly posted welcome, alt.sex.femdom is a "climate in which those with a common interest in the somewhat unique sensibilities of female dominance could freely and comfortably discuss their views, fantasies, opinions, experiences, and information."

Over 20,000 people regularly read alt.sex.femdom, and as women are held in the highest esteem in this newsgroup, men are "forced" to be on their best behavior. "Jay Doubleyou," the group's founder, advises new alt.sex.femdom readers to avoid "categorizing a woman as a dominant simply because she posted here, keep disagreements polite and civil, and avoid sending 'wannas' (unsolicited requests to enter into a relationship), since a dominant female looking for a partner is more than capable of making her own specific intentions very clear." GIFs, JPGs, binaries, and other large files are not welcome here, as these image files require a significant amount of storage space and may discourage sites with limited storage capabilities from picking up the newsgroup.

One man asks, "What are some polite, tasteful ways to let a dominant woman know of her power" and his "eager willingness to adapt to her needs." He has tried "a shy smile, looking down in deference" when their eyes meet, "searching for ways to please her, and remaining focused and attentive to her when other attractive women are around." "Tammy Jo" proffers a technique used by one of her submissives: "When I offer my hand, one of my occasional bottoms [bottom refers to the submissive partner] gently touches it to his lips with downcast eyes, releases it, and steps back giving me a shy glance and smile."

"Ipsofac," a 42-year-old divorced self-described handsome professional man posts a personal ad seeking a "self-confident woman who wants a man to please, worship, obey, and live according to her dictates and become a reflection of her perfection." A man, posting from an anonymous mail site in England, is "willing and able" to give himself "in body and soul via e-mail or in person to any member of the superior female sex for her pleasure."

According to the group's welcome post, the components of female dominance may include any of the following aspects: adoration, aggressive sex-play, alternative spirituality, body worship, bondage and discipline, cruelty, denial, depersonalization, domestic service, dominance and submission, erotic boxing/wrestling, erotic "torture," feminist spirituality, fetishism, flagellation, foot worship, "forced" feminization, "forced" chastity, Goddess worship, gynosupremacy (female superiority), humiliation, maid service, personal services, role playing, service, and subservience.

As a newsgroup still in its infancy, alt.sex.femdom is doing an admirable job keeping its objectives and principles intact. But beware if you're a female who dares to post here, you'll be besieged with e-mail from subservient males eager to serve you in every conceivable way. After I placed a post asking for information, I was flooded with e-mail. I am still mulling over the tempting offer of free "maid service" with no hanky-panky, offered by a banking executive. But then again, he hasn't seen my apartment yet. Only the inclusion of hanky-panky could keep that level of cleaning passion alive!

∽

Rugged the breast that beauty cannot tame.
—John Codrington Bampfylde, "Sonnet in Praise of Delia"

alt.sex.breast   In a world where strip clubs promoting dancers with 80-inch bust lines are doing smashing business, it is no wonder that the Internet too indulges in mammary overload. alt.sex.breast is devoted to all forms of breast-related discourse, from brassiere analysis to the pros and cons of small- versus large-bosomed women. One man, admitting he "needs to get a life," uploaded about 40 biblical verses containing breast references.

In answer to requests for "teat icons for X Windows," and "GIFs or JPGs featuring breasts," the newsgroup's FAQ includes an assortment of bosomy graphics. However, as a rule, there are no graphics uploads permitted on the newsgroup.

The unofficial court jester is "Evil Carlos," who frequently interjects strange breast-related comments or questions. "Is it true that you can tell the color of a woman's nipples by the shade of her lips?" he posts. "Are there any black women out there with pink nipples?" he inquires. "And what about those little bumps around the nipples? What are those for?"

Breast oddities are brought to the surface. "I saw in 'World News' a picture of a woman with three breasts. The third was neatly placed in between the other two in perfect proportion. Does anyone else know of any women with more than two breasts?" posted a multiple-breast lover.

A thread entitled "How bra size is measured" elicited a flood of replies, one of them a scientific analysis from "James." "A noted neuropsychologist uses breast/testicle asymmetry as an index of hormonal levels and relates this to degree of cerebral laterality," James writes. "The degree of asymmetry varies slightly over the year with testes, and over the month with breasts." The outpouring of bra-size-related discourse propels "Karen" into posting, "Why do so many people feel a need to write about bra sizes? I realize I'm not male, and therefore there are some things about topics that interest men that I just won't 'get,' but this one is a total mystery to me. Why are there multiple posts every day about how bra sizes are measured?" "Norska" replies, "Men are simply trying to translate the different sizes they see into an equation (thus balancing the visual and scientific parts of their brains) so they can discuss their preferences intelligently. Therein, instead of yelling 'I love mondo hooters,' they can yell 'I love 44DDs' or 'I want a 34B.'"

"William" wonders how strip-club dancers and porn stars "get those large breasts. After all the publicity about the ill effects of implants, why would reputable plastic surgeons perform an operation to inflate these women to an HH or so?" The perils of silicon and saline implants are then bandied about for weeks.

In response to a man who made it clear that he used breast size as a dating barometer, "Dyson" responded that he cares less about the breast size of women he loves than about a "warm smile, lovely eyes, loving heart…. This group exists because breast appreciation is something of a 'taboo' practice. One can walk up to someone on the street and offhandedly say 'you have a nice smile,' but if you said 'you have nice breasts,' you'd be missing teeth in no time."

The occasional personal ad appears in alt.sex.breast, such as the one from "Larry," an adept nipple torturer. "I torture nipples sensually, mixing pain with pleasure. I'd be interested in e-mail from women describing what they like best in NT (nipple torture) or TT (tit torture)." Or "Idabra's" post asking for "lactating or pregnant pen pals for exchanges of ideas."

Although this newsgroup was started just in the past six months, it has already built a loyal following of men and women. Naturally, the majority of posts are from men, as the entire Internet is male top-heavy, but a surprisingly large number of women post on alt.sex.breast, often puncturing inflated male mammary-oriented stereotypes.

Some posts from alt.sex.breast

alt.sex.breast

2Ø5 messages have been posted in the last 14 days; You've read none of them.

[2Ø5 messages in 62 discussion threads]

1 Busty Wall St. Wonders! (2 msgs)
2 WEENIES (2 msgs)
3 Nipple Color (8 msgs)
4 Bra Sizes (1Ø msgs)
5 Do women like men's nipples? (1Ø msgs)
6 More than 2 breasts ?? (21 msgs)
7 Sagging Breasts (4 msgs)
8 Talking Tits (8 msgs)
9 cosmetic vs natural on Tuesday
1Ø Love those LARGE breasts (2 msgs)
11 Lacy confections for larger breasts...
12 How is bra size measured? (2 msgs)
13 Huge artificial breasts (3 msgs)
14 Nipple Colors (*)(*)
15 Difinitive third nipple sampler...(here)
16 Love Small Breasts (2 msgs)
17 Biblical References to Breasts
18 Been caught starin', sorta.
19 Nipple Torture in the SF Bay Area
2Ø 3rd nipple = death by fire. (2 msgs)
21 Best Breasts
22 3rd Nipple (3 msgs)
23 Sensitivity and Other Things (3 msgs)
24 Space For Rant: Small-Breasted Women Unite
25 Nipple Question III (4 msgs)
26 Huge Breasts (6 msgs)
27 mothing

~

alt.sex.voyeurism   Voyeurism and exhibitionism appear to be likely bed partners in alt.sex.voyeurism, as the discussions frequently include both sides of the naked coin. Tips and techniques of the trade are eagerly posted, such as the latest in secret listening and viewing devices. Many folks provide intimate details on their voyeuristic activities. Others seek their own special voyeuristic soulmate by posting personal ads.

One man, posting from an anonymous mail server, passed along details on a favorite hotel. "The Sheraton Twin Towers in Boston is absolutely the best place for the voyeur in all of us. The hotel is two towers that face each other, and I've had successful viewing pleasures many times. Often, at around 11 p.m., flight attendants check in from the Boston airport. One night a very attractive blonde stewardess came into her room directly across from mine. She slowly removed all her clothes, and with the aid of my binoculars I could tell she was a natural blonde." His post was greeted with enthusiasm, as reflected in a follow-up post requesting names of "hotels across the country and internationally that provide a good view." A post recommending the virtues of a New York-based Sheraton encouraged another man to attempt to assemble a voyeuristic gathering of "two or three horny geeks with a telescope, spotting scopes, and shotgun mic willing to get a room and stake out the place for a weekend."

Others, such as "All-Eyes," seek to trade voyeur videotapes. All-Eyes is willing to trade his video which contains secret footage (shot through windows from across a courtyard) of a beautiful blonde who parades around her apartment scantily clad.

An anonymous male poster confesses that he enjoys watching men "jack off in the men's room." To better observe, he found a stall which had a toilet-paper holder removed, leaving four drill holes. He confessed to spending hours with his eyes pressed against the drill holes watching a parade of men masturbate.

"Andy" details his experience watching teenage girls next door. "I just got a telescope to view my next-door neighbor. She is a single mother with two kids, around 12 to 14. This afternoon I caught her daughter masturbating on her mom's bed. I feel like I got my money's worth the first day! I'm going to try to get a camera hookup to the telescope so I can take some pictures." His post elicited rousing enthusiasm consisting of "post the photos here" to "tell more details about how she masturbated and what the girl looked like." Another male placed a video camera inside a carry-on bag and placed the bag in the bathroom just before his girlfriend's cousin began her morning routine. The result was a tape with over 10 minutes of a "beautiful naked female toweling herself dry, drying her hair, and applying creams to her body." He then volunteers to upload about 25 stills to the newsgroup for everyone's enjoyment.

"Zoraster" posts a common voyeur thrill. "In the shopping mall, I passed underneath the stairs going up to the second floor. A young redheaded girl (about 16, still fresh looking but with curves) was walking up the stairs. I observed her walking up the stairs, and could see her pink panties nestled between her freckled thighs. And as she stepped from one stair to the next her panties shifted from side to side revealing her pubic hairs." However, as the girl reached the top of the stairs she paused and looked down, gazing straight into the voyeur's eyes. Zoraster was unflustered, smugly stating "little things like that make life a pleasure."

Although there are occasional interjections from law-abiding citizens appalled at the brazen illegal conduct of the self-proclaimed voyeurs, the tone of alt.sex.voyeurism resembles the fellowship men must share when they gang-bang a woman. There is a mob-run-amuck-type mentality that permeates this newsgroup and bolsters the collective voyeur egos. As a group, these men feel invincible, and alt.sex.voyeur is their collective feeding station, providing a continual source of virtually none of the daily recommended levels of humanity.

～

alt.sex.exhibitionism   There probably is a bit of an exhibitionist in all of us, explaining why we preen in the mirror before departing for work, making sure we look good from every angle, and why we don't just wear paper sacks as attire. However, the devotees of alt.sex.exhibitionism are a whole different breed, devoting their sexual life to displaying their natural charms to unsuspecting souls.

"Jazz" brags about exposing his genitals to the married hostess at a recent party and claims that "she didn't hide the fact that she was looking at my crotch in hopes of another glimpse." "Vader" posts that he enjoys driving "around Santa Monica naked" and surprising unsuspecting female passersby with a glimpse of his erect penis. "Bob" convinced his wife to try jogging nude in a quiet, secluded park, surprising an unsuspecting male jogger. His wife "agreed it was a turn-on experience."

Some folks move beyond shock value, and into someone else's pants. One man detailed his experience at an adult male theater house, where he masturbated openly, and then reached for a stranger's penis, and masturbated him to orgasm as well.

Along with the first-person exhibitionist displays are countless sightings like the one posted by "Melvin," who noticed a "lady walking her bicycle past the train station. Judging by her 'bounce,' she wasn't wearing a bra. As she passed, I turned and watched her walk away and noticed that her white dress was semitransparent and the outline of her white thong panties was clearly visible. Her exhibitionism made my day!"

Like everyone else, exhibitionists just want to be loved, resulting in a large number of personal ads on alt.sex.exhibitionism. "Scot" goes so far as to post his hotel phone number in search of a one-night exhibitionist stand with a "woman who likes to watch or be watched." Is he successful in his dating quest? Scot reports that his post elicited some steamy telephone sex, but no in-person visits. Now, if Scot were a woman, there would have been over a hundred phone messages and countless date requests waiting in the hotel!

Years ago, riding the #7 train, I sat alone, midday, in a subway car on its way to Flushing, Queens. Lost in my thoughts, I hardly noticed that a young man walked through the empty car and took a seat directly across from me. As I was reading my newspaper, I became aware of some moaning sounds. Thinking the man was wounded, I looked up to find the man masturbating himself to orgasm as he intensely scanned my face for a reaction. I remember feeling perplexed and a bit horrified that this man felt the need to "share" his experience with a total stranger. I was also scared. I leapt out of my seat and ran through the cars until I found an elderly couple sitting quietly. I sat across from them and breathed a deep sigh of relief. The danger was over. Minutes later, the door swung open and the public masturbator strode into our car. He took one look at the elderly couple, another longing look at me, and then passed on through the car.

My experience sheds light on a point left unattended on alt.sex.exhibitionism—how exhibitionistic behavior affects the unwilling participants. Reading through post after post from eager, proud exhibitionists, I'm awestruck at the overwhelming egocentric nature of these men. They demonstrate no concern for the unwanted images and fears they leave behind.

~

alt.sex.watersports   If you're looking for a newsgroup that discusses water polo, or sex in the hot tub, you're way off base in alt.sex.watersports. Although this newsgroup has seen more active days, and is riddled with snide commentary from Christian fundamentalists, there are still a "sprinkling" of folks engaged in discourse on scatology and golden showers.

A post from "toilet slave" offers his "service to anyone in the New Jersey area wishing to use a toilet slave," provoking "Geoff" to angrily reply, "What in Almighty God's name is wrong with you? You permit your body, created by God himself, to be depraved voluntarily by such disgusting filth? Does your perversion know no bounds? You are a sick individual, and I pray for you fervently." The rest of the newsgroup bands around "toilet slave," wondering aloud why a Christian fundamentalist is subscribing to the newsgroup at all. Geoff replies that he stumbled upon the group out of curiosity, "wondering how such wholesome activities as swimming and waterskiing could be perverted with a foul sexual component."

One man explains the dearth of activity in alt.sex.watersports. "I believe one of the greatest reasons for inactivity in any area is the fear of prejudgment. There are many people who make a sport of judging what others do within the scope of their private, consensual, sexual sphere of life. After so much bashing, many people tend to stay away." He continues: "Why should a person be forced to defend their personal preferences and choices day after day? Putting an e-mail out under one's real name can be scary. One can't help but wonder, 'What if my boss finds out? What if someone who knows me, who I haven't shared this side of my life with, reads this?' When a person is getting fired at, some defend, some suck, and a good number run until the 'shooting' is over. alt.sex.watersports is, in my opinion, a victim of bashing."

Despite the taunts and digital jeers, this fetish group marches forward on the search for like-minded players. "Watersport" seeks girls who are ready, able, and willing to take photos of themselves while in the midst of a "BM," (bowel movement) as he refers to it. However, people writing personals are generally directed to place them in a more appropriate area, such as alt.personals.fetish.

"Spanky" subscribes to the newsgroup because he was looking for a way "to become interactively involved with someone, or a group, sharing [his] particular interests." The anticipation of meeting someone new, or encountering an old friend, keeps him glued to the newsgroup.

According to the newsgroup's FAQ, "Watersports is a slang term for the practice of passing bladder fluid to enhance sexual intimacy, or in other words, erotic peeing." The FAQ does not focus on watersports's place within dominance and submission games, preferring to focus on "the sharing of something intimate and personal between individuals who are emotionally bonded and trust each other, and who seek to deepen their bond and their trust with this special token of their love."

~

alt.sex.strip-clubs   Everything you ever wanted to know about strip clubs is laboriously and meticulously uncovered in alt.sex.strip-clubs. Although there is no formal FAQ for the newsgroup, enthusiastic strip-club aficionados have taken up the cause of providing regional FAQs that list and rate the local area clubs.

Many women wonder why men frequent strip clubs. Not surprisingly, no women ever post here, but they might find the answer to the question interesting. A man, posting from an anonymous mail server, as do the majority of posters here, pontificated, "There are plenty of people who prefer professionals for a number of reasons, e.g., cost (one-time fee vs. relationship maintenance costs), variety, skill level, etc. Not to mention that it is probably hard to find a friend who will purchase sexy clothing and strip for you without expecting something back."

According to one poster, "A strip club is one of the few places that men can be unabashedly male." Another man states that he is an "art lover" who enjoys watching pretty women put on a show, and it "doesn't matter where you get your appetite as long as you eat at home." "Equitus" enjoys the unadulterated ogling. "Walking down the street, I often mentally undress attractive women, but I'm much too polite to stare. At a club, I can *really* look, and don't have to mentally undress them. I find this satisfying."

The majority of the newsgroup is devoted to men offering their grind-by-grind assessment of particular strip clubs. One man critiqued a club in Ontario, Canada, commenting that the "girls were older than God, one needed a shave more than I did, and the two decent-looking dancers were colder than liquid nitrogen."

Interestingly, a post from a man inquiring "what to talk about" with nude dancers resulted in an avalanche of posts. "Treat queens like whores, and whores like queens," posts one man. "Look them in the eye, instead of at their chest," posts another. "Engage her in appropriate small-talk conversation, never ask about her home life, income, sexual persuasion, and other overly personal questions." "Act like a gentleman, as they're used to jerks." Another man rebuts everything that was posted before, stating, "Strippers are interested in one thing and one thing only—money—so if you've got a lot to flaunt, you're their best friend; if not, you're just wasting their time."

"Bill" suddenly becomes aware of the dearth of "nude dancing girls on the Internet" and asks everyone to do their part in encouraging dancers to become wired. "How about joining my campaign to get more dancers on the Internet?" Bill cheers. "If you have an obsolete modem lying around, why not ask your favorite dancer if she has a computer, and if so, offer to install the modem and get her started on-line?" "Jeff" responds that the women may face a "security risk" by posting on-line, stating that a digitally equipped stripper friend "has had problems with loonies" and every "dancer who's worked awhile has her share of stories about guys stalking them."

The talk goes beyond where to get the best jiggle and flash, to where to find the best lap dance money can buy, and which places have "specialty" rooms where patrons patronize the dancer's orifices, as well as their dance routines. Not surprisingly, the newsgroup is a mecca for folks who want to underhandedly advertise their own establishments in the guise of an enthusiastic patron. One such post elaborated on the "superiority of Bangkok" women versus American, enthusiastically recommended taking a "Bangkok Love Tour," and provided the tour's contact phone number and address for additional information. He posted that "you take a girl home who is more beautiful than you've ever seen in the States.... You make love, and she stays all night, and even shows you around town the following morning. When you send her home, you pay the equivalent of $25 to $40 U.S. However, lots of guys never send her home. Many guys take her back to the States!"

~

alt.sex.magazines   The library of magazines—more commonly "sticky" than not—are categorically discussed, examined, and analyzed on alt.sex.magazines. Are there porno magazines available from the Indian subcontinent? Where can one find magazines featuring big, stocky gay men? What is the difference between *Cherry* and *Cheri* magazines? Did anyone get an advance copy of *Penthouse* featuring a stripped-down Tonya Harding? Answers to these questions, along with many, many more, can be found in this newsgroup.

In one of the more entertaining posts, "VideoSan" provides his "2¢ worth regarding men's magazines" using a "strokability" rating system. Of the 17 magazines he reviewed, *Swank*, featuring "girl-girl and girl-guy pictorials in explicit poses" and *Cheri*, featuring hard-core photos and steamy features, provided VideoSan with the highest "strokability" rating at 4.5.

Some posts from alt.sex.magazines

89 messages have been posted in the last 14 days
[89 messages in 28 discussion threads]

1 Adult Images (2 msgs)
2 SPLOSH!
3 LYL? (2 msgs)
4 What do women see in men anyway? (15 msgs)
5 women look better naked (was Re:What do women see in men anyway?) (24 msgs)
6 New Rave
7 The Polished Knob
8 NTSC<->PAL conversion done.
9 Tailends (2 msgs)
1Ø Cherry/Silken Locks wanted
11 Anti-Censorship Organizations Sought
12 international.. (2 msgs)
13 Adult and Erotic Cards
14 JULIA PARTON!! (2 msgs)
15 Playboy query
16 Circumcision
17 Tonya Harding X-rated Penthouse Photos described
18 Electronic Obscenity (14 msgs)
19 Looking For...
2Ø Looking For.../Correction
21 Asian American and Asian European "Porn" Stars (3 msgs)
22 Tonya Harding Pics
23 Cheri back issue
24 Comments regarding various mens' mags (2 msgs)
25 Penthouse email address?
26 Tonya in Penthouse (2 msgs)
27 Playboy address?

~

alt.sex.fetish.diapers "Just got home from work," posts "Goodnites."
"I took off my man clothes and put on my diapers and plastic pants.
Gosh, it is so relaxing." "Submissive sissy-boy, 30, brown hair, clean shaven,
in diapers and pink plastic panties, seeks skilled Daddy-Master with nice
face and good body capable of doling out bare-butt spankings, verbal humiliation," posts "Diaper-Slave." "Twenty-something white female into
all aspects of infantilism enjoys playing the role of a little girl in diapers
and plastic panties, seeks new diaper pen pals," posts "Diapered Brat,
Melinda." If you think you've stumbled into an alternate universe, you

just may have, for alt.sex.fetish.diapers is the Usenet's Romper Room for the business set.

alt.sex.fetish diapers provides a forum for people with interests in infantilism, diapers, age-play, and related activities. According to the group's FAQ, "Here is a place where people can get in touch with their feelings and interests, so they don't feel alienated just because they have an interest that" isn't mainstream.

Infantilists experience sexual pleasure from being treated and/or acting like a baby—such as being bottle- or spoon-fed and having their diapers changed—within the context of role-playing. They may enjoy wearing diapers, using diapers to catch body eliminations, and wearing adult-sized baby clothes such as bibs, pacifiers, and baby bottles.

According to the FAQ, "Infantilism does not involve minors in any way, shape, form whatsoever. Any discussion of activities involving minors is totally unacceptable for this newsgroup. We are here to celebrate childhood, not to spoil it and make it a living hell."

Alternate universes require alternate resources, and alt.sex.diapers.fetish is chockful of answers for the inquiring adult baby. If you can't find diapers to fit your 40-inch waistline at your local drugstore, alt.sex.diapers.fetish provides mail-order companies that carry the latest in grand-sized diaper wear and provides step-by-step instructions for dying plastic panties in any color of the rainbow. If you're interested in trading your copy of *Phantom of the Opera* for a video of *Phantom of the Diaper*, this is your newsgroup. For the isolated, disenfranchised infantilist seeking to join the diaper liberation movement, there is DPF (Diaper Pail Friends), a California-based organization dedicated to helping infantilists and diaper fetishists.

~

alt.sex.fetish.feet   If Jodie Foster only knew the lust her dainty feet stirred in some foot-fetish (FF) men, she might consider a job change. First, she was worshipped by John W. Hinkley, Jr., and now scores of foot-obsessed men labor over her every step, going far beyond her screen movements, and spinning obsessive bondage-related tales about her feet and toes. Star foot worship is a popular theme in alt.sex.fetish.feet. Some current popular foot icons include Fran Drescher, AKA *The Nanny*, the QVC shoe model, Cybill Shepherd, and Tanya Tucker.

The FFs post their foot sightings, creating a walk on the wild side out of seemingly humdrum scenarios. "Stephen" describes a scene in the movie, *The Mask*. "One scene in the middle of the flick involved The Mask dancing with the gangster's girl in a nightclub. He kisses her, and the camera pans in to a shot of her feet, and her shoes fly off from the force of the kiss." "Hang 10" alerts the group to recent foot shots of Julia Roberts seen in *Rolling Stone* magazine, and rates them a thumbs-down. "I'm afraid her feet only scored about a 12 out of 100, and she could have used some sexier sandals, too."

Sean Young's appearance on *The Tonight Show* created an uproar within alt.sex.fetish.feet. "Turk" exclaims: "God, I hope someone got her appearance on tape! She walked out barefoot and pregnant and said her feet hurt. Jay offered to rub her feet for her, and she kicked both her feet up in Jay's face. Jay rubbed her bare feet throughout her first segment! I have it on good authority that Sean's hubby is very much into foot play." "How could I have missed it," cried a disappointed FF. "Please someone provide the video," panted another foot fancier.

"To paint or not to paint" toenails is a debate that heatedly rages in alt.sex.fetish.feet. "Sam" admits to "ditching a girlfriend because she refused to stop wearing purple nail polish on her toes. Brightly colored enamel is a distraction from the natural color and shape of the foot. How can one enjoy the shape of the toes, the gentle curve of the arch, the firm roundness of the sole, if one's eyes are locked on the harsh paint." "D.R." disagrees, posting that he finds nail polish a "big turn on" and is attracted to "strong, vivid hues. There is nothing quite like a woman with fluorescent orange polish on her toenails."

FFs frequently place personal ads in search of the ultimate, dream feet. "Hari" is looking for a white woman, 20 to 30 years old, who is willing to let him "massage her beautiful feet." "Tony" seeks "beautiful women with sexy feet," requesting that interested peds send photos of their feet for review.

alt.sex.foot.fetish goes beyond the foot to examine the role of the shoe as well. One post tells the story of a man and his shoe. "You envision the shoes as the woman you want to be seduced by. Looking at the shoe, you see the sensuous lines, the curves in the shoe, and the creases in the leather, as the curves and lines of a woman's body. The exciting outline of the interior of the shoe frames that which represents the vagina of the woman you're seducing. You slide the shoe over your ever-hardening penis, slowly pumping yourself into the shoe, gently reaching for the inner lining toward the toes, your balls gently surrounded by the leather of the heel of the interior of the shoe. As you feel the shoe and begin to screw this fantasy woman, you want to smell her aroma and touch her skin. You reach for the other shoe of the pair, and smell the aroma of the well-worn sensuous woman's shoe. The combination of the aroma and the physical contact is so exciting that physical ecstasy is inevitable."

Some are more interested in what feet can accomplish. "Stego" is interested in "viewing videos featuring severe, vicious trampling, that is, as rough as it can get." One man recollects his indoctrination into the trampling arena. As a child, he would sneak under the kitchen table as his mother and her girlfriend sat chatting. He'd proceed to remove the shoes and socks of his mom's friend, lay on his back with his legs directly under the chair, pull back his shirt to expose his bare stomach, and place the woman's feet on his abdomen.

Many foot fanciers have developed advanced foot theories. Sam recounts that "just from my observations, I've been able to create a theory. Women who care the most about themselves have the best-looking feet (void of calluses, bunions, etc.). It is the women who care what others think about them—and demonstrate this by packing their feet into tiny shoes—who wreck their feet."

Some posts from alt.sex.fetish.feet

alt.sex.fetish.feet

188 messages have been posted in the last 14 days;
[188 messages in 123 discussion threads]

1 Sighting in the classroom (5 msgs)
2 JODIE FOSTER STORY (2 msgs)
3 pretty feet (3 msgs)
4 alt.sex.tickling
5 oops
6 Jodie Foster request
7 Hands
8 General difficulties with Re: Turkbros Files
9 tickle group
1Ø foot tickling
11 When did you start liking feet?
12 more on shoes
13 COLOURS !
14 PICS
15 A LITTLE HARD...
16 Difficulties with Turkbros files
17 Looking for Jan. '79 Penthouse
18 cable sighting
19 Hooray for Tickling Newsgroup! (2 msgs)
2Ø How to Get ASFT
21 Looking for Story in a '81 Penthouse (was Looking for Jan. '79)
22 the mother of all sightings (2 msgs)

～

alt.sex.fetish.amputee   "Carol has just announced that her newest video will feature a bilateral above-knee amputee named Carla," posts an amputee enthusiast. Every kink has a place on the Internet, and a lust for limbs lost is no exception. "I've been turned on by amps since I was a child," posts "Carlos," "and I'm at a loss to explain why." Carlos goes on to ask if there's a place where "amp fetishists can meet with actual amputees in a context where the amputee would not be creeped out by the fetishist."

His plea is answered. Another poster informs him about a magazine entitled *Fascination,* a quarterly special-interest magazine catering to unusual life-forms and pairings. This low-volume newsgroup discusses amputee-related fantasies and experiences, the latest in amputee-featured movies, relevant lifestyle magazines, photo exchanges, and amputee-positive gathering spots, both on- and off-line. Amputee fetishists relay their fantasies and experiences with amputees. "Wizard" is mesmerized by a one-legged woman who stands ahead of him in line at a fast-food restaurant. "What struck me most of all about her, was that her right pant leg was rolled up, not folded, to above where her knee would have been! I watched to see if any leg remnant would twitch within, but it was not to be seen. I longed to catch her attention and strike up a conversation, but my SO was waiting for me out in the car."

Some of the posters go beyond amputee adulation to "wannabe" status. "Mike" posts that although he does not want to purposefully sever a limb, he is a "leg brace and crutch wannabe." He is interested in hearing from others who "were amputee wannabes and are now amputees...people who've done what it takes to be what they feel they are."

Even amputee enthusiasts take issue with Mike's zeal regarding voluntarily dismembering body parts. "Phaedrus" responds, "Why would you want to cut your leg off if you didn't have to? Get some gumption and find some happiness within yourself no matter what your lot in life is. If you're unhappy now, cutting off your leg won't help. Imagine how you'll feel the next day when you think, 'Holy shit,' what have I done? Doctor, is it too late to reattach?'"

～

alt.sex.fetish.fa

Subject: Gainers?

Newsgroup: alt.sex.fetish.fa

I'm wondering if there are any gainers out there. I'm 27, 5'8" and 530 lbs. That's right, 530 lbs., it's not a typo! I love being fat, and I want to gain even more weight. I know there are others out there who feel the same. Let's make our voices heard!

Chubby chasers rejoice! alt.sex.fetish.fa is here to meet all of your girth-loving needs. This is not the newsgroup to voice complaints about being too fat, or where to find advice on dieting. In fact, if you dared post about your trials and tribulations on a weight-loss regime, you'd be flamed unmercifully. alt.sex.fetish.fa embraces fleshiness in all its glory. Men and women post personal ads seeking corpulent lovers and the men drool over photos of scantily clad or nude 250-plus-pound women.

Fat men and women post about fat acceptance. "Big Michele" states that she is "30 years old, 5'5", and 400 lbs." She states that she spent much of her life "ashamed" of her appearance, and "was always on the wrong side of the jokes." Today, instead of hiding behind tent dresses, she prefers to wear only form-fitting bright clothing. The new clothes, and the confidence the new smiles and lustful stares inspired, gave Michele a new attitude filled with confidence and self-respect.

alt.sex.fetish.fa has lost ground and membership to the more general alt.sex.fat forum. According to "Mark A.," "The vast majority of FAs do not consider themselves fetishists, or their preference a fetish because the source of their admiration is a person, not an object. This feeling is one of the reasons why this newsgroup has basically been abandoned in favor of alt.sex.fat, which is a more general group and opens up the conversations to fat persons as well as FAs. The fact that this newsgroup is located in the 'fetish' subgroup does nothing to advance legitimate acceptance of FAs as regular, normal folks who simply would prefer having a fat partner." Related groups include alt.personals.fat, alt.personals.big-folks, and alt.support.big-folks.

At a time in history when fat bashing appears to be one of the few socially acceptable discriminatory activities left, this newsgroup, as well as the other four fat-related groups which demand body acceptance, are a welcome addition to the diverse Usenet community.

~

alt.sex.fetish.fashion   "Fetish": *Webster's Ninth New Collegiate Dictionary* defines it as "an object or bodily part whose real or fantasied presence is psychologically necessary for sexual gratification and that is an object of fixation to the extent that it may interefere with complete sexual expression." If you've read alt.sex.fetish.fashion long enough, inevitably almost every area of fashion and clothing has devoted fetishists eager to wear, touch, or play with the desired object.

alt.sex.fetish.fashion was created by Per Goetterup, a computer science student at the University of Copenhagen, on October 27, 1993, to "spread the knowledge about fetish fashion and dressing for pleasure; what it is, why we wear it, where to get it, and so on, and to show that fetishists are not perverts, weirdos, psychopaths, or worse. Fetishists are simply regular people with a special taste in clothing and/or footwear."

According to the newsgroup's comprehensive FAQ, which is regularly uploaded on alt.sex.fetish.fashion, as well as found in news.answers and alt.answers, "All kinds of people are into fetish fashions, from secretaries, editors, housewives, students, to politicians and the unemployed. Some people only wear their fetish fashions to fetish parties or while engaging in a scene at home, while others wear something along with regular clothing on a daily basis, to 'stay in touch' with their fetish." The major topics covered in the FAQ, as well as on the newsgroup, include fetish materials, namely leather, PVC (polyvinyl chloride), spandex, and rubber; sexy footwear; fashion designs using the aforementioned materials; the "art of depicting these fashions; bodypainting; stories relating to all of the above, both fictional and true-life anecdotes; and related fetish literature, comics, music, movies, and TV."

The group requests that all binaries be posted in alt.binaries.pictures.erotica.fetish, but many people fail to comply, as this new fetish binary newsgroup is only carried on a fraction of the Internet sites. Hence, a quick stroll through alt.sex.fetish.fashion finds over 25 fetish photos out of 160 total posts. Since the D/s (Dominance/submission)and B&D (bondage and discipline) crowds often incorporate dressing for pleasure as a related part of their lifestyle, it is not surprising to find that many of the posts relate to this lifestyle.

Although this is a sexually oriented newsgroup that deals with an area widely considered deviant or taboo, the group conducts itself in a professional, courteous, and helpful manner, which can only aid in smashing myths that portray fetishists as misanthropes.

∽

alt.sex.fetish.hair   If the terms "crew cut," "flat top," "buzz cut," and "brush cut" set your hair on edge, alt.sex.fetish.hair is your digital salon of choice. Combing through the newsgroup, you'll see posts concerning anything and everything related to tresses. At least half of the posts are photo files featuring everything from head shots of sultry, long-haired redheads, to girls holding a shampoo bottle, to girls curling each other's hair. There are few photos of hairy men available, however.

Hard-to-find hair-centric videos are all the rage on alt.sex.fetish.hair. "The new Barber Shop video is the best haircutting video I've ever seen! One scene shows a young guy requesting a mohawk. When the mohawk is perfected, the man asked the barber to cut off the mohawk and shave his entire head! The barber clips off the brush, goes over his head with an edger, a safety razor, and then a straight razor. At one point the man has his eyes closed and is just enjoying the feel of the razor. Very hot," posts "Clippers."

The color of hair is carefully analyzed and examined on alt.sex.fetish.hair. "I was never turned on by redheaded women until this year," posts "Bob." "All of a sudden, I became attracted to redheads, and now I can't get enough!" "Rio Mario" agrees, stating, "I never liked redheads either, but four years ago I found myself in class next to the most beautiful woman, and she had pale perfect skin and a huge mass of red hair! I found myself taking classes just to be in the same class as her!"

Hair on body parts other than the head is also enthusiastically discussed. Rio Mario posts that he came across a "cashier who was wearing a top cut 3 inches above her navel revealing a thick patch of hair stemming from her pubic region" and was surprised she displayed her hairiness in all its glory, but concluded that "maybe she had an unusual insight into what a turn-on it was!" The pro-female-body-hair lifestyle is well-represented on alt.sex.fetish.hair, with organizations such as Hair Apparent regularly posting information about their organization and newsletter.

"Coyote" states that he realized he had a hair fetish after weeks spent reading alt.sex.fetish.hair. "The part of my fetish that gives me the most pleasure is shampooing a female's hair, or just watching a female's hair being shampooed. Are there any GIFs of women being shampooed out there?" "Mike," burdened with a fetish-buster wife, is looking for a female to cut his hair in a "fetishist-significant manner."

All in all, this group is a relatively low-bandwidth newsgroup that provides interesting insight into a relatively esoteric fetish. However, a word to the wise: After reading the newsgroup for a while, you'll never look at your hair salon the same way. Now you'll wonder if that man or woman staring at you during your haircut or shampoo is really a closet hair fetishist desperate to sneak a peek!

~

alt.polyamory   If you believe one is nice, but two or more is infinitely better—that is, in terms of sexual satisfaction—alt.polyamory is the place to explore this hedonistic side. According to the group's FAQ, written by "Elise," alt.polyamory was founded by Jennifer Wesp on May 29, 1992, to discuss the trials and tribulations of loving more than one person simultaneously. "Polyamorous love may be sexual, emotional, spiritual, or any combination thereof…and is also a descriptive term used by people who are open to more than one relationship, even if they're not currently involved in more than one."

How come bullets aren't flying out of jealous rages? As one female polyamory devotee states: "The key in defining polyamory is openness, having multiple relationships with the knowledge and consent of all partners rather than by deceit. A great many people have secret affairs while they're in supposedly monogamous relationships. Those people may have the potential to be polyamorous, but are not practicing polyamory."

As explained in the comprehensive FAQ, the orchestrations of polyamory are so diverse as to induce dizziness. "'Primary' is often used in a hierarchical multiperson relationship to denote the person to whom one is most strongly bonded. 'Secondary' follows from primary, and denotes a person one is involved with without the strong emotional, legal, or economic bond. A 'Triad' or 'triangle' refers to three people all intimately involved with each other equally, and 'Vee' is three people where the structure puts one person at the 'hinge' of the vee, also called the pivot. In a vee, the arm partners are not as commonly close to each other as each is to the pivot."

There's also "line marriage," a term taken from science fiction writer Robert A. Heinlein, meaning a marriage that from time to time adds younger members, as spouses die off at the same rate that younger replacements come aboard. "Polyfidelity" is a relationship with more than two people who've made a commitment to keep the sexual activity within the group, and not have outside partners. Last but certainly not least are the "quads," "pentacles," and "sextets," who exist in multiple arrangements with more than three members. Wheew! You need a calculator and word processor to keep track of all possible polyfolk computations.

This very active newsgroup discusses and analyzes every aspect of polyamory, from the emotional, legal, and economic complexities to how to cope with questions about the unusual lifestyle. Not surprisingly, there is a sporadic post from a heterosexual male looking to live his fantasy out with a "hot, bi babe." These actual "hot, bi babes," tired of being viewed as a "spectator sport," lampoon these hormonally charged men with prickly, blistering flames until the male is suitably ashamed and undoubtedly retreats back to the world of "hot, bi babes" video rentals.

In answer to a query of what one would "call a person who wants only one partner, but the partner may have multiple partners," "Dave" replied, "a sucker." "Don's" rebuttal was swift and piercing, "Does it occur to you that not everyone shares your needs, or sense of 'equalness'? Several people have described being on the 'I don't need/want more than one partner, but it's okay that my partners do.' None of these people are gullible, stupid, or easily duped. You insult them by inferring they must be to have allowed themselves to be in such a situation."

"Karen" sums up her views on polyamory eloquently. "I don't do monogamy well. I'm lousy at it. For me, it's like a suit that doesn't fit. I can't get what I want in a monogamous relationship, and a large part of that is, what seems to me to be, ownership agreements. I don't like taking responsibility for another person's sex life, nor do I like how I feel when I'm restricted by agreements, nor the way I act toward that other person."

Live polyamorous banter can be found on the "polyamory" channel on IRC. People interested in subscribing to a very active mailing list devoted to supporting this lifestyle can write to triples-request@hal.com.

How does one know if someone is in the "lifestyle"? Is there a secret handshake or something? "Not that I know," states Elise. "However, there are several proposed symbols, of which the most common—and the most humorous—seems to be the parrot!!"

~

alt.sex.masturbation   "Why are you always knocking my hobbies?" Woody Allen's character complained to Mia Farrow's in *Hannah and Her Sisters* after she expressed concern about low sperm count potentially due to excessive masturbation. "At least it is sex with someone I love," he continued. Self love is the purest form of love according to many regular posters on alt.sex.masturbation.

The heart and soul of alt.sex.masturbation revolves around the posting of anecdotal masturbation experiences. Sooner or later, every conceivable masturbatory tip and technique is covered within this newsgroup. For example, do some men have more fun with fruit than with actual flesh-and-blood sex partners? Is there more to the phrase, "Here honey, have some watermelon," than meets the eye? One anonymous male posts about his love affair with a watermelon. "First, I bought a watermelon, made a hole in it (better use a sharp knife to get the hole round enough), and then I removed some fruit flesh with a spoon. After that I put the cold melon on the desk, held it in place, and started to fuck it. And believe me, the melon can be much more satisfying than what most women are carrying with them. The feel and sounds it makes are like the real thing. It was so exciting that I pumped my sperm inside it after five minutes. The second time I did it to a melon, I placed the table diagonal to the TV so I could see screwing from the VCR."

Some people misconstrued the VCR comment, mistakenly thinking the man videotaped his fruit frolic, and begged for copies. Another man wondered whether the melon lover "foisted off the melon on some unsuspecting poor soul afterwards." "Stern" remarked that this all "puts a whole new meaning on the term, 'Melon Head.'"

"Jamall" recommends "humping the mattress. Insert your erect penis between a firm pillow and the mattress, keeping your chest on the pillow, and hump your ass." Another man explains how he pleasures himself while wearing pantyhose and claims it is "no more addictive than without pantyhose."

"Hardon," who apparently has spent too much time watching *This Old House*, recommends using a power sander as a sexual aid. "At the highest speed," it takes him "just a few minutes" to orgasm. He recommends removing the sandpaper to "minimize the friction" and pressing the soft backing against the penis, so that it is caught "between the vibrating attachment and a smooth surface."

Although there are few women posting on alt.sex.masturbation, the male populace appears to be equally divided among straight and gay and bisexual men. Interestingly, men who claim they are straight, often masturbate in concert with other men. "JWheeler" defends this practice by stating that while they masturbate, they "always watch a porno" and "never look at each other." People frequently post about upcoming "Jack & Jill" gatherings, which are coed masturbation sessions.

It appears that there are no adult-oriented newsgroups that are immune from Bible-Belt proselytizers. One rants, "When the day of judgment comes for you, and it will, you will stand before GOD ALMIGHTY and review your MASTURBATORY PRACTICES, and He will cast you asunder and into the GNASHING JAWS OF THE DEVIL." Judging from the imaginative incorporation of ordinary household appliances, clothing, food, and assorted other miscellany into the masturbatory act, it may take a power as great as God to keep a masturbation-proof house. Could be, though, that the Great Almighty is hip, or at least immune, to the practice of self-pleasuring. Maybe His mind is on war, famine, and violence. Or maybe He's on the Internet musing, "How do they think of this stuff?"

Some posts from alt.sex.masturbation

alt.sex.masturbation
[4Ø9 messages in 175 discussion threads]

1 Circle "J" in Boston/New York
2 Strokin' Dick at The Bijou (2 msgs)
3 Chest Hair (4 msgs)
4 Let's talk about dick
5 New Service: JPEG delivery via E-Mail
6 White stuff squirts out of penis (12 msgs)
7 Ball Stretching
8 ..... Texas ..... I will shave 18-21ish ..... experienced (2 msgs)
9 Sex Toys (3 msgs)
1Ø Favorite/Most Dangerous Public Places?!? (3 msgs)
11 in the tub
12 Making safe toys.
13 Survey: Car Sex (2nd post/repost) (8 msgs)
14 Old greek style to do it (4 msgs)
15 female videos?
16 Get a Forced Haircut While JOing
17 Have any of you guys tried bisexuality? (2Ø msgs)
18 JACK AND JILL CLUBS IN THE UK?
19 SM 38 ISO (mannish?) F
2Ø sleeping nude
21 underwear (1Ø msgs)
22 masturbation technique (3 msgs)
23 I've masturbated for a go
24 Frequency of Masturbation
25 I am atracted to men. Am I gay? (2 msgs)
26 (PLEASE CUT IT OUT) Re: TOP 1ØØØ X-RATED VIDEO
27 A year's worth of masturb
28 Ever caught someone masturbating? (6 msgs)
29 Anybody caught? (19 msgs)
3Ø Penis size? (12 msgs)
31 Your absolute favorite way!!!!!
32 I've masturbated for a good year now I have a cuve (2 msgs)
33 On line now for jo 1:2Ø mdt (2 msgs)
34 Hot Live Chat! >>>1-8ØØ-34Ø-8877<<<
35 Menstrual masturbation (4 msgs)
36 Astroglide (lubricant) - WOW! (3 msgs)
37 15 Years old or under
38 freeway chicken choking (2 msgs)

~

alt.sex.necrophilia   Wake up and smell the decomposing bodies, Moral Majority! The Moral Majority and the Christian fundamentalists, who spew negativity and eternal damnation throughout the gay-oriented newsgroups, have chosen not to voice any contrary sentiments at all in alt.sex.necrophilia. However, there is a hard-core group of Internet free-speech advocates who staunchly defend alt.sex.necrophilia and post fond hopes for its continued good health. "I hope that the assholes, bigots, and hypocrites leave the necrophiliacs alone. However, I don't think I'll be here very often," concludes "Clayton." "Reverend Mrzlak" advises fellow posters to help keep alt.sex.necrophilia a secret as the "feds are already doing some heavy work in alt.sex.pedophile and are hip to the scourge of kiddy-porn." His signature file proudly exclaims that he's been "sucking putrefying titties since 1975."

Necrophilia, the ultimate taboo, is discussed in a very low-bandwidth way on alt.sex.necrophilia. It is difficult to ascertain whether the posts are simply sick, perverted jokes, or if they are based on reality. Let us all pray that some people merely have very active and warped imaginations, and that it goes no further.

Reading through the posts, it is impossible to discern fact from fiction, sick jokes from warped reality. "Mofo" posts that he is unable to tell whether this is all "for real or not, but on the off chance" it is, he asks how necrophiliacs get "consent," and what the "attraction" is, and if there is a "term limit on the age of the corpse., i.e., a few hours, days, or years?" His question is never tackled and answered by anyone admitting to necrophiliac tastes.

The closest anyone comes to admitting necrophiliac tendencies are the stray posts from a man claiming he likes to have intercourse with dead dogs, and has the GIFs to prove it, and men who post an affinity for the gothic look. "Davey" posts that he once sat next to a gothic girl at a bar who was clad in all black, with whitened skin, dark hair, and heavy eye makeup with blood red lipstick. Her "sunken eyes were accentuated with rings of dark makeup," which inspired Davey to blurt out, "I think necrophilia is gross, but in your case, I'd make an exception." She smiled.

Isn't sexual intercourse the ultimate union of body and soul? Do we merely make love to bodies, unconcerned about the spiritual inhabitants? The necrophiliacs, or wannabes, who frequent alt.sex.necrophilia seem to place no sexual importance on the value of a soul, as the bodies they'd most like to seduce are decaying shells, whose spirits have since departed.

~

alt.sex.telephone

Subject: A Plea for Phone Sex...

Man with digital tip wishes to meet woman with analog ring.

Object: telephony

Few of the men who troll through alt.sex.telephone are as clever as James, but they all pursue one common goal: hot, steamy, uninhibited phone sex. Whether they're after sultry phone sessions with anonymous strangers, or the heavy breathing and orgasmic sighs of a long-term phone mistress, the men who post on alt.sex.telephone are thoroughly turned on by the integration of Mr. Ear and Mr. Hand.

Although the majority of posters are male, occasionally a female "delurks" and makes her opinions known. In response to a man's concern that a love of phone affairs is not enjoyed by women as much as men, "Mikki" replies, "I think someone should make the distinction between sex-with-strangers-on-the-phone and sex-with-someone-you-know-on-the-phone. The majority of posters on this group are men who are most interested in having phone sex with total strangers. I had hoped this group would include valid discussions about the wide variety of phone sex available, not just the mystery caller syndrome."

Men frequently go so far as to actually post their residential phone number in their personal ad phone partner quest. "Judith" wonders aloud if this methodology reaps results. "I'm rather bemused by the recent flurry of posts from men soliciting phone sex, and posting their phone numbers. I know if a woman did that, she'd be besieged by numerous calls. So tell me guys, have you had any luck?" No success stories were ever posted in response to that question.

Only "professional" women post their phone number in alt.sex.telephone, that is, phone sex operators in search of business. It would be unsafe for the average woman, who simply enjoys telephone sex, to post her phone number on the Internet. According to Mikki, "The safety factor is important. I would feel trepidation about giving my number to someone I met on the Internet. In the past, I've given out my phone number to men I've met through business associations on-line. Even within that dull context, I was besieged with unwarranted, personal solicitations."

"Todd," a radio host and telephone sex aficionado, relays how phone sex has been erotically interwoven in his life for two decades. "My high school sweetheart and I worked out regularly on the phone as a tension release and contraceptive aid. I met my first wife on the phone, and it led to phone sex. I've had phone sex with countless female listeners, as I suspect most male radio personalities have…. I'm married again, but this has not stopped my attraction to the genre. There are two kinds of phone sex, just as there are at least two types of real sex: detached (with strangers) and intimate (with your SO or SOs). I've experienced the same heartache when a particularly amazing phone relationship ends as I do when a real one ends. And I get just as disappointed to discover that a woman who does great phone is otherwise vapid, as much as finding out an attractive woman is a dull conversation partner."

alt.sex.telephone was founded in the summer of 1994 by "Aaron" (aaronilk@netcom.com) to fuel his personal passion for telephone erotica. Aaron, himself, is on a quest to find the perfect phone sex partner. No one-night phone romps for him, however. "I'm really not interested in any more one-timers. I'm really hoping to meet a nice young female with a nice voice who is into the mutual masturbation style of phone sex. I am interested in developing a friendship, but keeping it exclusively on the phone."

Hmm…the "mutual masturbation style" of phone sex? Are there different schools of thought on phone sex methodologies? According to Aaron, most definitely. "There are two distinct styles of phone sex that occur most frequently. There is the 'talk dirty to me, tell me what you'd do if you were here' variety…which bores me personally. If I wanted erotic fiction, I'd go read some. The second style is what I refer to as 'doing what comes naturally.' Mutual masturbation is my preferred method. This method includes all of the sounds we'd make if we were actively engaged in F2F (face-to-face) sex, although sometimes I'm even noisier on the phone if that is stimulating to my partner."

In the heat of the night, with only the squeal of a modem for company, many people are ready to reach out and touch someone via Ma Bell. The motives are varied—whether the impetus is the taboo of talking "dirty" to a stranger, temporarily escaping the boredom of "microwave sex" (fast, boring, convenient), a determination to practice the safest in safe sex, or reveling in fantasy role-playing—phone sex is alive and well and making new mystery lovers on the Internet. James D. Murray, co-author of *Encyclopedia of Graphics Files Formats*, eloquently sums up the allure of phone sex. "Phone/e-mail sex allows one to see the uninhibited side of a person first. The bonds that form this way can be much stronger than those formed by face-to-face meetings. Consider 200 years ago, when writing letters was the only way to communicate across any real distance. Relationships went on for months and years via the mail. Courtship letters have given us an intimate peek into the romantic lives of such notables as Thomas Jefferson, Alexander Hamilton, and Benjamin Franklin. One of my great joys is having a complete stranger for a lover. Terrifying if it were in person, yes, but quite safe over a wire."

~

alt.sex.enemas   "Coffee Connoisseur" prefers his home-brewed java served up in a bag, rather than a mug. "Wino" doesn't care if he imbibes red or white wine, as long as it's served at room temperature through a nozzle. Welcome to alt.sex.enemas, an alien world bursting with wet anal adventures and flatulent gastrointestinal odysseys.

Just how far does an enema travel in the intestinal tract, and how much fluid can be administered without doing any serious damage? What other types of fluids can be injected into the anus besides water, soapy water, diluted wine, and beer? Is there anything that can be mixed as part of an enema that will suppress the urge to evacuate? If these questions themselves have not caused you to "evacuate" from this chapter, alt.sex.enemas is your one-stop enema information resource center.

Posters provide tips and techniques on every aspect of enema administration, as well as share enema-centric erotica. "Master B" posted an enema-driven fantasy tale which began, "Over the months, Marie had grown past her initial capacity, while learning to contain the water. As she took her water, she watched as her belly stretched with the weight of the enema, conforming to the increasing volume. The very warm water melted away any resistance inside her."

Sometimes humanity cries out to be loved in alt.sex.enema. "Howard" is looking for a Chicago-based woman who is looking for a relationship that would "include giving and receiving enemas."

Also featured on the newsgroup are photos of men and women in the act of giving or receiving enemas. These photos often inspire lusty thanks. In response to a photo of a bound woman receiving a blue-colored enema, "Theresa" posts that the photo "got my husband's attention, and I soon benefited from that.... I think that vaginal plug is actually a breast pump, designed to milk new Mommies so that Daddy can get out of bed at 4:00 a.m. and feed Junior nutritious milk...although mine never did.... OUCH, my husband just reminded me that he did get up to feed Junior in the middle of the night, and is now spanking me three times on each cheek to illustrate how many times he helped out."

People on alt.sex.enema post their first enema experience as eagerly as most of us describe our first sexual tryst. "Bob" posts that he "started with a syringe" when he was eight years old but "graduated to a bag fairly soon using a standard two-quart enema bag." Others are fascinated by the body dynamics precipitated by engorging the anus with quarts of fluids, and proceed to measure themselves. "Jonathan" reports that his measurement of the largest part of his abdomen went from a pre-enema state of 32½ inches to post four-quart enema status of 35½ inches.

The discussion of new anal materials is always welcome here. An anonymous poster reports that he tried using a banana. "A banana is SO nice because it feels like a turd, it's self-lubricating, and it gives that nice, 'filling' feeling. I used a good cleaning enema until it ran clear, applied some lubricant, and then broke the banana into two pieces as each tapered end eases insertion. After dilating and pushing the banana firmly in place, I relaxed the sphincter and pushed the banana totally past the sphincter into place." Bob reports that Damiela tea "offered a somewhat enhanced feeling of voluptuous eroticism."

The intelligence level of the alt.sex.enema posters is high, and there are few, if any, judgmental outbursts. Digital voices are raised only to alert fellow enema aficionados about health and safety risks, but never to cast lifestyle aspersions. The newsgroup appears to include both straight and gay men and women and has not yet received the attention of the Christian fundamentalists.

~

alt.sex.girl.watchers

From: Darksoul

Subject: Girl watching

Newsgroup: alt.sex.girl.watchers

Every heterosexual guy I know watches girls. It usually goes something like this:

1st Guy: Holy Shit! Check HER out!

2nd Guy: Wow! She is STACKED!

1st Guy: Yeah, and nice ass too.

2nd Guy: Damn, I could bang that thing all day!

<Repeat 5ØØ times>

Why we need a newsgroup to discuss the above event is beyond me...unless it is aimed at discussing stalking, fatal attractions, etc.

Now that the male bimbo has taken Madison Avenue by storm and women can be titillated by a passing parade of muscular men strutting around in their underwear selling everything from beverages to clothing, why isn't there an alt.sex.boy.watchers newsgroup? Is it because as soon as the newsgroup were up and running, it would be overtaken by NAM-BLA (North American Man-Boy Love Association) members like moths to a flame? Could be, or maybe there aren't enough sex-starved women on the Internet yet to warrant a boy-watching group. Or perhaps the women are too busy keeping men at bay, and don't want to start a newsgroup that shouts, "TALK TO ME, I'M LOOKING TO TREAT A MAN AS AN OBJECT!"

Although a newsgroup named alt.sex.boy.watchers might warrant attention from the FBI, alt.sex.girl.watchers has not elicited any special notice. Many men who post infer that "girl" refers to any underage female, and proceed to post fantasy after fantasy on pedophile seduction.

The rest of the group, who interpret "girl" as "woman," offer up tips and techniques on "babe watching." "Mike" and his friend have created an "entire babe watch language" they can "freely use without raising suspicion of the 'babage' in question." If one of the guys "thinks a potential babe is spotted," they use the "term J.A. or Jerk-around Alert, or in some cases it means Juvenile Ass." They use their own special code like, for example, #3 J.A. L means "three J.A.'s to the left." "Max" posts that "malls and airports" are the best places to scout babes. "I think the first thing I see is their general figure. I next flick up to their breasts and then, to the most important area of all, their faces."

Others complain about the perils of girl watching, that is, that girl watching leads to girl longing. "Rolaids" works at a major software store where only a fraction of the customers are female. "It is always funny to watch my fellow employees drooling over the sporadic babe who comes into the store. The annoying thing is that they almost always come in with a boyfriend or husband. It is so frustrating to watch the few women that do come into the store prance all over the place driving me crazy, and know there is nothing I can do about it."

The best place to watch real, live women is not on your computer. If that is your ultimate quest, turn off your computer and journey outside. And remember, women can hear boys mumbling silly catch-attention phrases like "J.A. to the left," and think the only people who utter such signals have not yet evolved along the human evolutionary chain.

～

alt.sex.spanking   In a nutshell, alt.sex.spanking is "bondage lite." Once Madonna publicly admitted a few years ago that she liked her rump to be paddled occasionally, spanking entered the slightly-to-the-left-of-mainstream world of sexuality and became Middle America's kink.

Many of the people who post in alt.sex.spanking are also frequent posters in alt.sex.bondage. This newsgroup includes techniques on safe spanking, caning do's and don'ts, the occasional misdirected personal advertisement, and lots of fictional stories with "Spanky" front and center.

"Marlo" comments that caning (using a rod to administer beatings) makes "great fantasy stories, but when done in reality, it is very dangerous." "Debbie" concurs, posting that "canes are pretty serious play, and it certainly takes skill to know how to use them. The welts can take a long time to heal." She adds that while the pain was severe, she's never gotten any scars from any canings she's had. "Dave," on the other hand, posts that "caning can be exquisitely sensuous in the right hands. Sometimes after a fairly sound spanking, the spankee may be a bit numb, but still seek more sensation—the cane can provide a little extra 'zing.'" "Netrider" is also pro-caning. "We use a very thin bamboo cane about 3½ feet long. The small impact area combined with the longer cane makes for a very good lick on my wife's bare bottom with only a light swing."

alt.sex.spanking is less flame-ridden than its older brother, alt.sex.bondage, and the general tone is warm and accepting. If you are interested in getting your feet wet in milder aspects of dominance and submission, or if you're a diehard spanking enthusiast, alt.sex.spanking may provide the punishment you've been looking for.

$\sim$

alt.sex.intergen   NAMBLA (North American Man-Boy Love Association) posts their latest press releases on alt.sex.intergen. Men post about the philosophical differences between loving and having sexual intercourse with, versus just raping a 12-year-old boy. If you really want to get a glimpse into the pedophile's mind-set, read the posts on alt.sex.intergen. The men's signature taglines are subtle, yet say volumes. "Ajay's" Internet signature reads, "A closeness to nature is the only key that can open the doors to innocence." "Raoul's" signature is "Fight abuse, not sexual feelings!"

The modus operandi of the pedophile is available on alt.sex.intergen. "As a kid, all I saw was the repression and guilt adults tried to force-feed," writes "Bill," a frequent poster. "I swore I'd never act like that on a kid, and would never force kids into anything. Most of all, I was not going to repress their sexual feelings like most adults did, and do. I divide the types of pedophiles into three varieties: the ones that get hard-ons forcing kids to do something against their will, the ones with loving feelings toward children who allow the possibility it might grow into something consensual and mutually pleasant, and the ones who have these feelings but who would never act on them due to fear of negative repercussions from society."

Another pedophile describes his upbringing as being positive and without abuse. He states: "My sexual attraction to young girls is not mutually exclusive. I am nearly as attracted to adult women. My pedophilia was not caused by any abuse, and probably wasn't caused by a specific incident. I simply have it." Another man voices similar sentiments: "I think pedophilia is something one is born with, like homosexuality, and I don't feel the need to be 'cured.'"

Pedophiles posting here commonly attempt to justify their sexual love of children. "Punisher" posts, "I think there is a big difference between someone who forces his or her sexuality upon someone else, and someone who has consensual sex, even if that 'someone else' is a minor." "Uncle Fester," one of the few contrary voices on alt.sex.intergen, takes issue with "Punisher's" logic. "Just like the big difference between a drunk that drives under the influence and a drunk that doesn't, right? They're both drunks, but the qualitative difference between a pedophile and a child molester is that the former has not yet been arrested. In fact, the pedophile is simply at the larval stage of child molestation. The adult holds all the responsibility in sexual relationships with a minor. It's a 'power' relationship and we all know who wields all the power."

"Vinnie" says the "idea of engaging in sex with a minor is morally reprehensible. Anyone who thinks otherwise could not possibly have kids." "Stinkfoot" responds, "No, what's morally reprehensible is that you DO have kids and are apparently unwilling to share." Deep shudder and shake. alt.sex.intergen represents one of the most morally repugnant newsgroups on the Internet, and its only value is knowledge. Knowledge is power and perhaps, armed with inside knowledge about a pedophile's rationale and plan of action, we can help protect our children.

∽

alt.sex.erotica.marketplace   Are you looking for the perfect gift for the man who has everything? Well, how about appeasing his submissive side with the "Dominatrix Wall Calendar," or satisfying his aural side with "Earotica," a collection of erotic audio recordings? alt.sex.erotica.marketplace is one-stop shopping for the erotically inclined. If you're looking to buy used panties, looking for a discreet place to get those photos developed of your husband posing in a teddy, or the latest in adult CD-ROM software, you'll find it available for a price on alt.sex.erotica.marketplace.

All of the adult-oriented Usenet newsgroups are filled with posts advertising everything from used adult magazines to dildos. When the advertising traffic becomes ridiculously high and strays off the conversation topic, someone inevitably stands up to the commercial onslaught and cries out, "If you have something to advertise, please post it in alt.sex.erotica.marketplace!"

The majority of the posts are simply advertisements, with the occasional thread delving into related issues, like the specific laws and regulations relating to mailing adult products across state lines.

Parents may be surprised at the entrepreneurial high-tech ventures their children are pursuing while tucked away at college. "Sarah" posts, "Hi, I'm Sarah, and I sell photos, slides, videos, and special items via mail order. Personal service guaranteed. There are 13 girls available and we're each students here at the university. Phone sex is available too, as well over 18,000 slides and photos of us featuring tons of oral sex. Blow jobs are our specialty!!"

~

alt.sex.pedophilia   Not surprisingly, alt.sex.pedophilia is not carried by the majority of Internet providers. However, after numerous attempts to access the newsgroup on dozens of on-line services, I was able to access the group through Delphi. I queried, "Does this group actually discuss having sex with children?" "Bill" responded that the group's focus is as follows: "One person will post flamebait. Idiots take the bait. Other people make fun of the idiots. Real pedophiles try and convince everyone it's OK to boink pre-pube kids. They get flamed. That about covers it."

Bill is on target with his cogent assessment of alt.sex.pedophilia. All of the pro-pedophilia forces who post hide behind anonymous mail servers. This group, more than most, receives a lot of posts from unattended terminals such as the one from "Eric," which stated in part, "when I was 7 years old, I was raped by a big fat sloth of a woman named Tasela. She threw me down in her trailer on the bed and tied my hands to the bedpost. I was so scared that I shit in my pants. She proceeded to eat my defecation out of my underwear." This post—obviously a warped prank—infuriates the newsgroup, and many people attempt to finger his account. "Bob" takes the opportunity to grandstand from his digital post. "You are a good example of what happens when fear, anger, hatred, and ignorance are left unchecked."

The only interesting aspect of this newsgroup is that it still exists on some level and is being distributed by a minority of Internet providers. While it may have served as a feeding ground for pedophiles in the past, all that remains now are a few stale crumbs, soon to be swept away.

～

alt.sex.movies   Why do porno babes wear high-heeled shoes all the time? Did Cindy Brady "do" Opie? Do the Brady Girls swallow? Has Marina Sirtis, from *Star Trek: The Next Generation*, done any pornos? If this is the kind of burning question that keeps you up at night, alt.sex.movies is your source for adult movie information and folklore trivia. What kind of people frequent the alt.sex.movies newsgroup? According to the group's FAQ, written by the founder Jim Knapp, "People in the alt.sex.movies newsgroup, are, on average, very well-adjusted people who think the viewing of pornographic materials is, in the worst case, harmless, and in the best case, enlightening and enjoyable."

The rumor about Marina Sirtis doing porno movies actually was given birth in the Internet's rec.art.pictures.erotica newsgroup, where someone posted a topless photo of Marina Sirtis being whipped by another woman. The person who posted it identified the photo as originating from a mid-1980s thriller, *The Wicked Lady*. This movie was rated R, but was not a porno movie by any stretch of the imagination. However, rumors started to circulate fast and furious that this photo was indeed from a porno film. According to Knapp: "Soon afterwards, an anonymous picture was posted showing Marina Sirtis performing oral sex on a man. If one looked at the picture closely, it was obvious the picture had been faked. The body didn't match skin tones with the head properly, and the mouth was open in more of talking fashion than any sexual position. Still, this picture was distributed widely, and the rumor that 'Counselor Troi' was a porn actress got its start."

Some of the more outrageous sexually explicit acronyms found on alt.sex.movies are unique to the newsgroup. DAP is digital shorthand for double anal penetration (two penises in one anus), DP is double penetration (one penis in the vagina, and the other in the anus); and DPP is short for double pussy penetration (two penises in one vagina).

alt.sex.movies maintains a World Wide Web (WWW or Web) server in Utah. (The Web is a hypertext linking system that connects machines on the Internet by subject matter. Web servers are set up by people who are interested in a particular topic, and who offer a one-stop informational resource on their topic of choice at their Web site.) "It's a pleasing irony that our WWW is established somewhere porn is virtually unavailable on the open market," reports Knapp. Their WWW features reviews, biographies of adult actors and actresses, a variety of lists, the FAQ, and other items of interest to the adult film devotee. The address to the alt.sex.movies Web server is html://www.xmission.com/~legalize/asm/asm.html. If you're looking for the inside skinny on the porno industry, head to the alt.folklore.urban archive.

This newsgroup is a must-read for anyone who has an active interest in the world of adult films. Given the raunchiness of the subject matter, the posts are generally rather civil, and flame wars are few and far between. "If you want to engage in flame wars, head to alt.flames. We're not interested in your flames here," states Knapp. alt.sex.movies has posters ranging from married men raising children, to male and female college students, to the occasional oddball character.

～

alt.sex.stories, alt.sex.stories.d, and **rec.arts.erotica**   While the art of storytelling is as old as humankind, the instant gratification of digitally transmitted sex stories is a phenomenon of the '90s. alt.sex.stories is a totally unmoderated forum where anything goes. You'll find stories featuring bestiality, scatology, bondage and discipline, rape, gay sex, and even a sporadic appearance of old-fashioned vanilla sex. The rec.arts.erotica moderator uploads each story to the forum after reviewing it for acceptability. "In practice, most messages submitted to rec.arts.erotica are acceptable. By far the most common reasons for rejection are grammar, spelling, and formatting errors. While I correct some of these, an excess of any of them is considered grounds for rejecting a submission," states the moderator.

Few subjects are considered taboo on rec.arts.erotica. "Most sexually oriented material is acceptable here," adds the moderator. "This includes heterosexuality, homosexuality, bisexuality, transsexuality, bestiality, BDSM, fetishism, and so on. The sky's the limit. However, material with gratuitous brutality or nonconsensual activity, without literary value, may be rejected. I accept articles about rape and other nonconsensual activities because if I were to draw a line at where 'unacceptability' begins, I would imply that I regard the material I do approve as 'acceptable.'" Therefore, reading through the stories, you'll find the keywords *rape* and *nc* are used to highlight more violent submissions.

alt.sex.stories.d is where people go to talk about the stories posted on the erotica forums, alt.sex.stories, and rec.arts.erotica. "Lyn" posts, "There are very few females posting stories. A lot of the male-written material contains a lot of the cliché 'big dick, hot cumming' stuff in it…and when will the word 'clitty' become passé?" "Megan" writes, "Maybe we should take a poll among the women here. Thus far, I've heard only one person say one particular man could write convincing female characters." "The Flying Pen" takes exception to gender generalizations. "Bad writing is bad writing. It's not gender-specific. But I'm not saying that there is an abundance of good writing on alt.sex.stories. Most of what is posted is shit."

alt.sex.stories and rec.arts.erotica best serve people who crave erotic story-lines addressing a special kink that is rarely explored in mainstream erotica outlets. The majority of stories are amateurishly written and offer limited sexual suspense or plot. However, a few stories are absorbing enough to melt even the most frigid reader.

Following are the keywords that are most commonly used. Sometimes there are variations of these, but most of them are usually easy to figure out:

animal	bestiality and animals
bond, b/d	bondage (physical restraint)
dom	domination (primarily psychological)
ff	female-female contact
furry	sentient non-human characters (e.g. "Journal Entries")
gothic	vampires and other Gothic subjects (e.g. "Night Music")
group, mff, mmf, other combinations of m and/or f	group sex and threesomes
heavy	"heavy" forms of bdsm
incest	incestuous relationships
mf	male-female contact
mild	"mild" forms of bdsm
mm	male-male contact
nc	non-consensual situations
pedo	pedophilia (pre-pubescent) (e.g. "Misty")

poem	poetry
rape	rape scenes and other violent non-consensual sexuality
scat	scatology and coprophilia
sf	speculative fiction: sci-fi, heavy fantasy, and the like
sm	sadism and masochism
teen	consensual sex involving teenagers and postpubescents
trans	crossdressing and transgendered material
water	watersports and urophilia

alt.pantyhose   In a society that idolizes the garters-and-stocking-clad women of the Victoria's Secret catalog, it is a surprise to come across a newsgroup that idolizes the common pantyhose. "Why isn't this group called alt.stockings—aren't stockings a whole lot sexier than pantyhose?" I posted. One man replied that he personally finds stockings sexier, but that "many posters to alt.pantyhose think pantyhose are more alluring."

Not surprisingly, alt.pantyhose frequently tackles the pantyhose versus stockings issue, with female respondents generally praising the practicality and comfort of pantyhose, and males decidedly mixed, as males are not particularly concerned about the practical side of hosiery. "Gordon" compares the introduction of pantyhose to the demise of sexy legware. "Discussion about stockings versus pantyhose" results in the "fair gender engaging in a lengthy tirade on how stockings—these hideous, obscenely misogynist articles of fashion—were foisted on a compliant womanhood, and that no man could possibly endure their agonizing discomfort for a 15-minute period. This comes as a stunning surprise to those C/Ds [cross-dressers] among us!"

Gordon provided an entertaining, informative, and accurate description of alt.pantyhose:

> Here's how it works: Someone posts an erotic story in which pantyhose play an integral part. Somebody else bitches about it. Somebody else posts something about having sex with another man while at least one of them is wearing pantyhose. Somebody else bitches about it. Somebody posts a JPEG, GIF, or MPEG featuring attractive, pantyhose-clad females. Somebody bitches that the photos are of poor quality. Three

people bitch that they missed the scans, or screwed up the download and ask the original poster to post them again. Ten people ask, "How do I turn these funny characters into a real picture?" A flame war commando from alt.syntax.tactical shows up. People bitch at the commando. After about a week, all of the people who bitched at the commando start bitching at each other, because each one thinks the other didn't bitch in the accepted manner. Someone bitches about the people from America Online. The AOLers bitch back. People bitch first at one side, then at the other side, then at both sides. The expression "killfile" begins appearing more and more often. After awhile, someone posts something that might have a legitimate reason for appearing in a newsgroup entitled "alt.pantyhose." Someone bitches that the person who posted the item referenced in the previous sentence simply doesn't understand the scope, purpose, and function of this newsgroup.

Readership of alt.pantyhose is comprised of three main groups: women who seek advice on hosiery, men who like to see women in hosiery, and men who like to wear hosiery. There is a high crossover element from the alt.sex.fetish.feet newsgroup.

Is it a mistake to lump alt.pantyhose with all of the other sexually oriented Usenet newsgroups? The majority consensus from alt.pantyhose runs overwhelmingly towards pantyhose being sexual icons. According to "Pete," a self-described "pantyhose PHanatic," "I don't see what purpose pantyhose have other than sexual. They're not a 'practical' garment, and many women don't enjoy having to wear them every day, especially in the summer. ...I can't think of any other garment that is more strictly regulated by 'gender' than pantyhose, and I can't believe that's simply by coincidence. Pantyhose are such a highly charged sexual garment that I believe there's much more going on here than the major media would ever dare admit."

～

alt.lycra   Men in tights? According to alt.lycra, heads turn at the provocative sight of a muscular physique obscured only by a skin-tight Lycra (spandex) bodysuit. Are most of these men bold enough to wear Lycra in public? "LTT" posts that he often wears tights in public, and receives "mixed responses, but, surprisingly, never homophobic remarks. Often people will look twice or longer than normal." Another man adds that other men flirt with him when he's clad in tights or spandex shorts, and the looks he receives can be "very sexually gratifying."

alt.lycra, created in August 1992 by Dan Mitchell, serves a core membership base that appears to be evenly mixed between gay and straight men, with sporadic female input. Men frequently talk about the sensuous tactile sensations of wearing Lycra. "Seamless" enjoys cycling wearing a black Lycra full body unitard in cool weather. The "feeling of the cool wind penetrating the snug Lycra is really amazing, especially when not wearing anything else."

Many men post about their experience donning Lycra for various science-fiction conventions. The experience of being Lycra-clad for an entire three-day weekend often empowers men to wear Lycra in the regular, mundane world as well. "Mysquito," a sci-fi convention regular, used the confidence he got at the conventions and "ventured out into the real world." Now, his standard outfit is a "sleeveless boat-necked or zippered Danskin supplex unitard covered with XXXL+ shirts, tees, or sweatshirts."

The flexibility and versatility of Lycra is praised so often it should make DuPont's ears burn. "Jay" likes the fact that the fabric can be slipped on easily without wrinkling, and "washes and dries quickly, and cools or warms" the body depending on the climate.

alt.lycra is a place where Lycra-lovers trade tips on the best Lycra mail-order houses, the best-fitting Lycra outfits, the latest fashions and how to wear them, and the sexual significance of wearing the fabric. If Lycra is your life, alt.lycra should be your home away from home.

Some posts from alt.lycra

alt.lycra

38 messages have been posted in the last 14 days; You've read none of them.

Select which messages: Unread, All, Date or ?> [unread]
[1;1H[2Jalt.lycra
Page 1 of 1 [38 messages in 19 discussion threads]

1 Where to look... (2 msgs)
2 Lint (2 msgs)
3 Guys wearing lycra for fashion (4 msgs)
4 Guys wearing Lycra for fashion (2 msgs)
5 Guys wearing lycra as fashion
6 Men Wearing 'Tards
7 Marcea: still alive?
8 Men Wearing 'Tards (Part 2)
9 looking for good lycra mail-order (4 msgs)
1Ø The Crow outfit (2 msgs)
11 Guys who wear lycra...it's o.k., really (3 msgs)
12 Clarification
13 CATS costumes
14 Sport Europa for nylon/lycra

∾

alt.irc.hottub   Reading through the threads on alt.irc.hottub is the closest many of us may come to reliving (or ever living) our raucous, carefree *Animal House* days. Most alt.irc.hottub participants are 18 to 25
years old, and college-oriented, with the occasional gifted high schooler
or socially retarded 30-year-old. People that mix and mingle on the
IRC's "hottub" channel use alt.irc.hottub as their own digital billboard
to alert fellow bathers about parties and events, or just to engage in public flirting and/or humiliation.

The threads have little or no meaning to anyone outside of the hottub chatting circle. The posts are comprised entirely of inside jokes, subtle
asides, and personal disclosures. According to "Derek," a habitué of both
the Usenet IRC group and the IRC channel, the IRC hottub channel is
filled with both "normal" people and those with "some kind of mental de-
ficiency that the hottub fills. Many people aren't socially adept, and IRC
provides a way for them to express themselves, and live out fantasies."

Derek notes that there is a dark side to the digital dalliances. "Some
people get trapped in an imaginary world, and it becomes their only
social outlet. One girl I know moved to Washington from Wisconsin to
be with an IRC person she 'fell in love with.' It didn't work, and months
later she moved to Virginia to be with another IRC lover, and again,
within a month she moved back home. A desperate girl, she was not
able to find happiness in life, searched on IRC, and failed to realize that
it *is* still real life behind the screen."

However, the core focus of alt.irc.hottub is party planning. Young
people travel hundreds, sometimes thousands, of miles to meet their
IRC friends and lovers in person. "Winterhawk" announces a party four
months in advance. "The party location will be in Kenos, Wisconsin, in
an old farmhouse, so we can be as loud and raucous as we want. This is
going to be the party of a lifetime!"

∾

alt.clothing.lingerie   Any woman who has ever seen the twinkle in her man's eye as he spots the latest Victoria's Secret catalog knows the intrinsic power of lingerie. Silk, satin, and even rayon and polyester take on a level of significance unfit for sheer fabric. Or does the tactile and "eye candy" appeal of scanty underclothes go beyond the actual garments, and really reflect a desire to live a life carefree and sexy enough to warrant wearing—or enjoying the sight of a lover in—silk charmeuse boxers, teddies, garter belts, or merry widows?

In thread after thread on undergarments, the universal mind-set inevitably becomes one: Everyone starts imagining each poster sitting in front of his or her computer clad only in fabulous underwear. Many posters try hard to keep this illusion alive and percolating by ending their posts with an underwear update—Mike: "black Calvin Klein boxer briefs," Helen: "black satin jacquard string bikini and black stretch lace front close bra," or Joe: "just plain white boxers, still."

Interestingly, there appear to be almost as many women elaborating on lingerie as there are men who post reverential feedback. "It is so easy for you women to have us men panting and drooling by our monitors by sheer force of your simple lingerie descriptions," stated one underwear admirer. Surprisingly, you won't find a lot of binary photos here featuring alt.clothing.lingerie devotees scantily clothed. Posting photos publicly is actively discouraged, but encouraged as a private e-mail activity between interested parties.

Undergarment theorists abound on alt.clothing.lingerie. "Kiki" claims she can ascertain "what kind of underwear a guy wears on the basis of his personality" and cites an "accuracy rate of 80–90 percent." Just what are some personality traits that distinguish a person who favors one type of underwear from another? According to Kiki, "Boxer guys tend to be confident but not obnoxious, less frivolous, and not afraid of a little dirt and sweat."

Women use this forum to query men on their reaction to new lingerie fashions. "What do you guys think of teddies with attachable garter suspenders?" posted "XTC." This question elicits responses from women who complain they're too large-busted to find any of these garments that fit, and men who say their girlfriends are too top-heavy to wear this undergarment. "My SO has a 36DD chest and I can't find anything that fits her," grumbles "Christopher." "I'm lucky if I can find a bra in a nice color, let alone a teddy."

During September 1994, a lot of talk centered around the creation of an alt.clothing.lingerie calendar featuring photos of actual alt.clothing.lingerie posters. As many men volunteered to pose in their skivvies as women. Men and women ask about what they should wear. "Okay, I've agreed to pose for the calendar, but here's my dilemma," posts "Dave." "I've always worn standard white briefs, and want to use this calendar experience to expand my horizons. Any suggestions about what I might wear?"

"Zaid, size 34 John Henry briefs" has been mulling over the "function of underwear for a long time" and offers up some possibilities about the purpose of bras (such as "easing the back strain on women with big breasts" and "allowing women with small breasts to have a place to put stuffing in") and panties ("to prevent flashing everyone when you're wearing a skirt and catch a gust of wind").

"Mike," a poor unsuspecting soul, stumbled into alt.clothing.lingerie inquiring if anyone knows where he can get a "1969 SS Camaro body." "Kevin" responds, "More importantly, does anyone know where he can find a bra for it?" Somehow Mike's straying into the wrong newsgroup was the digital equivalent of the way most men look when they walk through lingerie stores: dazed, confused, and desperately trying to avoid eye-contact.

~

alt.hi.are.you.cute   *Cute*—what other four-letter word has such significance? Well, a few do spring to mind, but never mind. Just what physical characteristic defines "cute," anyway? Someone deemed cute by one, is labeled repulsive by another. Many women don't like being referred to as looking cute these days. That's an adjective reserved for little girls who sport pigtails and who jump rope. A lot of men don't take a shine to the cute label either. They are either very young, trying to look and act older, and bristle at the notion of appearing cute—which is the opposite of the worldly sophisticated look they're carefully trying to cultivate, or they're a Dick Clark type—older and perennially young and cute looking, but who would rather be thought of as dashing and handsome.

In any case, physical cuteness is all but irrelevant on the Internet, so most of the people here—who all appear to be from Generation X—attempt to generate a cute perception with verbiage. According to "Ben": "Real cute people don't just sit around talking about how cute they are. Real cute people expend some effort to write posts with substantive content, which would allow us to experience some of their cuteness, and offer a convenient outlet for our own cuteness. Saying 'I am cute' does not make a person cute, I'm afraid."

Ultimately, there appears to be only so much one can convey about cuteness, resulting in a low volume of posts in this newsgroup—

approximately 50 posts generated in two weeks. "I think to keep this group alive you would have to come up with a completely new subject," posts "Staffan." "There is only so much you can say about being cute. Beauty is a wider concept." Ben explains the low traffic of the newsgroup another way. "We're all just quietly basking in the glory of our own cuteness."

~

alt.party   Several years ago, while I was on holiday with several girlfriends, tucked away at a seaside Florida bar, the hunky bartender poured us all vodka shots "on the house," and asked if we wanted to "party" after closing. "Define 'party,'" was my retort. My girlfriends reeled with laughter, and the bartender turned many shades of scarlet, but never managed to articulate what "party" meant. My quest for a definition was sincere. It is one thing to go to a "party," and quite another to "party." Did it mean to kick back, get drunk, and sing camp songs, or did it somehow involve the removal of undergarments? I still don't know, and I'm not sure the alt.party newsgroup has aided in my decade-long search for an accurate definition.

Woodstock '94 is discussed, and the mud bath is relived in post after post. People query the group for hip party themes. "Don" posts: "I once went to a 'boxer' party where no one was allowed in, male or female, unless they were wearing boxers. People got very creative in their boxer attire."

Drinking games are analyzed. "'I've Never' is a self-paced drinking game that's aim is to unearth embarrassing information. Everyone has a drink. One person starts with a statement like 'I've never been to India.' All those who have been to India must drink one self-paced slug. If no one drinks, it means no one has gone to India, and the person that made that statement must finish his entire drink. All sorts of interesting things come out during the course of an 'I've Never' game. 'I've never slept with anyone in this room' is a favorite statement."

~

alt.amazon-women.admirers   *Attack of the 50-Foot Woman*, the classic science-fiction film, is the stuff of intense erotic fantasies for the hundreds of men who actively read the alt.amazon-women.admirers newsgroup. Although the 50-foot woman represents the amazon fantasy run amuck, the qualities that appeal to the giantess lover are larger than life: the amazon ideal is an athletically built, strong, muscular woman who is courageous and self-assertive.

alt.amazon-women.admirers was started in December 1993 by Jim Woodward, who also maintains the Amazons International mailing list as well as a California-based amazon-centric bulletin board, Amazon's Arena BBS. According to Woodward: "Amazons are physically and psychologically strong, assertive woman who are not afraid of breaking free of traditional ideas about and limitations of gender roles and femininity. In short, the classical ideal about mind-body harmony and unified strength—only extended to woman."

However much significance the true amazon-lover places in the spiritual perfection of his ideal, it is rarely discussed in this newsgroup. The main topic of fare is bodybuilding and weight-lifting championships—discussions centered around who measures up and why. At least 25 percent of the newsgroup is devoted to binary picture files featuring women with healthy biceps and washboard abs. A constant thread discusses the pros and cons of posting binary files in a discussion newsgroup. "Jimy" posts that he's "enjoyed the binary pics and the discussion" but feels "it's time to start a new group named 'alt.binaries.pictures.amazons' for the photos." "Mr. X" dislikes the "continuing balkanization of the Internet and votes to keep the pictures right here." "Mark" concurs, "This network is for the people by the people. Post the pix here, and let the naysayers go suck an amazonian-sized root!"

The rest of the newsgroup is devoted to amazon fantasy interludes. Some men post fantasies about being forcibly raped by amazonian beauties or the sheer thrill of seducing a brawny female. Whatever the story, the moral is always clear: Women dominate men in every area, and the men keep coming back for more.

What is the thrill of a giantess? Have some men finally grown tired of taking control, and are they turned on by being dominated by an amazon goddess? Perhaps. As one man posted, "It's a shame that there aren't more women who will take charge and say what they'd like to do for the evening or what they'd like to do sexually." Some men take adoration several steps beyond. A British man seeks an amazon woman "who wants to be worshipped, served, and serviced."

~

alt.society.underwear   "Sometimes I like to drive in my underwear," posted "Tammy." "I usually just slip off my skirt and drive home from work in my panties. The danger of discovery is the thrill. Once I got out of my car just with a shirtwaist covering my bottom, and two different neighbors made a point to mention they 'saw me come in from work the other day.'" According to the group's FAQ, alt.society.underwear was established July 1994 by Arnold Kasemsarn as a "forum to discuss society's views on underwear—what it means, how people react to it, and how the individual reacts to these views. People have widely different views about how underwear relates to their sexual and daily lives. Some people consider it merely underclothes, while others consider it an essential component of their sexuality. In any case, society, in general, discourages attribution of desire or anything else to underwear—leaving alt.society.underwear with a mission," states Kasemsarn.

The group's content consists of scanned pictures, stories, and true-life experience discussions. Do the vast majority of underwear references relate to female undergarments? "I really don't care much about men's underwear," answers Kasemsarn. "However as this group gets more traffic, there will undoubtedly be more discussions on male underwear as well."

The traffic jam *has* arrived on alt.society.underwear, and the drivers are scores of gay men. In San Francisco, the large gay male population has resulted in a plethora of fabulous male underwear shops. In much the same way, all this underwear talk has brought gay men on alt.society.underwear out of their proverbial drawers and eager to get the lowdown on briefs and boxers. "Mike" volunteers that his favorite pastime is "sniffing other guys' briefs...particularly if they've been worn all day." "James" admits he's been "known to walk off with 'forgotten' underwear from locker rooms and laundry rooms" and finds them "wonderful for masturbation." "Matt" collects used underwear and boasts a national collection stemming from New York, Pennsylvania, California and Michigan. Mike gets so inspired by the underwear talk that he suggests an underwear exchange group be founded.

Beyond incorporating used underwear as a sexual tool, the men on alt.society.underwear have proudly continued to respond to the Clinton-endorsed boxer versus briefs survey. "Jon" finds "boxers nice because they let in more air, but other times, when more security is called for, jockeys are preferred." Mike enjoys "letting it all hang out in the lazy days of summer...even if there's a protrusion here or a glimpse there."

Leave it to the British to take a historical look at underwear's evolution. British-based "Graham" notes that "closed-crotch female panties were only generally adopted within the past 150 years. Prior to this, women wore multiple petticoats, slips, or drawers that didn't join at the crotch."

"Jean" waxes philosophical on undergarments. "If they are called under-wear, it really means one doesn't wear them...that one simply goes around in underwear pretending to be naked. In effect, underwear is like little puzzles we all put around our waist." Underwear may indeed be like a puzzle, similar in that we're constantly trying to put all the pieces together in the right order to achieve the right balance between sensuality and practicality, and once that's achieved, we rip all the pieces off. And once a puzzle is solved and the mystery is over, it's time for some new underwear—oops, puzzles....

∿

alt.magick.sex   Wandering into alt.magick.sex, I expect to be greeted with post after post on Tantric sex, love spells, and mystically grounded tips and techniques on attaining out-of-body orgasms. With my notepad in hand, eager to jot down cabalistic rituals that ensure sexual serenity, imagine my disappointment in learning that 85 percent of the posts were nothing more than the tired America Online versus the rest of the Internet community flame war! Aren't mystical muses more evolved than your average Net flamebaiters?

It started with a proclamation from "Jon" stating, "Dear America Online Users, if you've reached this newsgroup by searching for 'sex,' you're in the wrong place. The newsgroup you're looking for is alt.sex.... Remember to read the FAQ message in any newsgroup to learn what is appropriate to post. alt.magick.sex is here for the discussion of sexual aspects of magickal work, and not for such things as personal ads and discussions of 'neato' positions. Considering the number of inappropriate posts by AOL members that I've read, I hope pointing them in the right direction will leave this newsgroup for true magick observers to enjoy." The floodgates opened with anti-AOL sentiment occasionally interrupted with more well-balanced outlooks. In response to a post which expressed disfavor about the "plebeians" running rampant on the Net, which used to be the "domain of the professional and educated," an America Online member charged that he was an "elitist motherfucker. The 'professional and educated' classes are not intrinsically superior." The squabbling grew in intensity until it consumed alt.sex.magick almost entirely, leaving people like "Joy," who complained that "there's hardly a thing in here that deals with the uses of sexual energies in the magickal environment."

However, the scant postings on the topic are well-written and interesting. "Anthony," an America Online member, writes that author Aleister Crowley defined Majick as "the science and art of causing change to occur in conformity with will." Anthony believes the term "will" was used by Crowley to denote, among other things, the love, urge, or drive that motivates the individual. "Crowley spelled it with a 'K' as reference to the Kundalini, a force which is said by the Tantric traditions of Hinduism and Buddhism to reside in the human body, lying dormant at the base of the spine in a form comparable to a coiled serpent, which when aroused, rises up the spine, illuminating the consciousness," Anthony wrote.

The petty bickering about the merit of AOL users was the impetus for many magick enthusiasts to mark alt.magick.sex in their respective killfiles. "Christeos" posts that "due to the lack of content in this newsgroup, I'm out of here. If anyone wants to talk magick, I'll still be scanning alt.magick." With the rise of magick as a valid practice on the fringes of mainstream culture, alt.magick.sex should be a haven for knowledge and enlightenment. Perhaps, once the tumult of America Online members accessing Internet services is over, the focus of this newsgroup will return and flourish.

~

alt.homosexual   In a two-week period, alt.homosexual, an extremely high-bandwidth newsgroup, generates over 1,500 posts. Currently, the most popular topic is gay male marriages. As a heterosexual woman, I find this interesting, as I've observed hundreds of heterosexual men do their best to escape what they perceive to be the monotony of matrimony. However, within alt.homosexual, hundreds of gay men are enthusiastic about the notion of legally unifying their life with someone else forever. Reading through the hundreds of posts, it is hard not to be moved by the level of sanctity and reverence they bestow upon the act of marriage. Of course, there is much more at stake here than simply thousands of gay men who are not phobic of lifetime commitments. Gay men who are involved in long-term committed relationships are simply seeking the same legal rights as heterosexuals—health benefits, home ownership, next-of-kin status, along with every other right that heterosexual married couples take for granted.

The same-sex marriage debate draws the ire of the conservative contingent, evident in great numbers on alt.homosexual. "Chucky," a former drug addict who spent six months in jail on drug charges, and who is now a devout on-line crusader against gays, has achieved almost mythic, cult-like status on alt.homosexual. In response to being referred to as "sodomites" by Chucky, some of the gay posters declare that Chucky must have been raped by a man in prison, thereby instilling his great dislike for gay men. Others speculate that Chucky is a repressed homosexual who needs to "buy a dildo and loosen up." The straight men who post in opposition to same-sex marriages believe that gay men are too promiscuous to make a lifetime commitment to one person, and that the sexual activities that they engage in are immoral and illegal. The gay men, in turn, spend a lot of time and posts bashing these stereotypical assessments, and occasionally reducing themselves to the level of the bashers by getting into the gutter and hurling inflammatory retaliations.

The straight men frequently post their belief that being gay is a life choice. "Ted" writes, "Gays make a choice to be homosexual in the same way alcoholics choose to be drunks. We are fairly sure that there is a genetic component that encourages some people to be addicted to alcohol. A series of choices must be made by the person who has that gene which includes taking the first drink, or else that person will never be an alcoholic. I believe that homosexuality is much the same." "Peter" responds that "substance abuse is not comparable to sexual orientation. Alcohol abuse can be compared to cocaine abuse, but there is simply no connection with sexual orientation.... Nobody can 'become' homosexual. Even if I were completely celibate, I'd still be gay...because my mind is programmed to be attracted to males and not females. My only choice is yes/no with respect to physical sex. My orientation is not a choice. Women simply don't produce the slightest twinge of sexual desire in me."

The tragedy of alt.homosexual is that there are so many gay issues that merit discussion, yet the majority of bandwidth is ultimately devoted to responding to antigay sentiments with catty comments, malicious rumormongering, and idle threats. Is it best to ignore the taunting jeers and post with dignity, or to flame back a response to every single insulting word? Posters reflect both extremes. A Swedish man posts: "How come so many people are obsessed with assholes like 'Chuck'? There will always be a few stubborn homophobes on the Net, as there will always be outlaws in the society. It's so depressing to see that most of the people posting to this group are full of nothing but hatred, personal attacks, and pure barking."

"Mike" posts that "ignoring the homophobes and rednecks will advance their status in pecking order.... When we are flamed, we flame back. When we are approached in a normal and friendly manner, we respond justly." Another poster disagrees, "We've lost sight of our agenda on alt.homosexual, and instead of creating a harmonious digital space, we've created a dysfunctional family that can't even spend the holidays together without squabbling."

Another very high volume newsgroup that discusses gay issues is alt.sex.motss (motss = members of the same sex).

∼

alt.transgendered

Transgender or Transgenderist—Someone in a state between genders, having made some changes (usually through hormones, etc.) and who does not wish, or in some cases, cannot have SRS (sexual reassignment surgery) and who therefore lives in the gender role of choice without surgery

TS (Transsexual)—One who does not identify with his or her anatomical gender

TV (Transvestite)—One (often heterosexual) who likes wearing clothes appropriate to the other sex

The acronyms used in alt.transgendered are unique to the transgender, transsexual, and transvestite culture. People post about their experience going MTF (male to female), or FTM (female to male), their SRS (sexual reassignment surgery), and bandy-about self-descriptive acronyms such as TS (transsexual), TV (transvestite), CD (cross-dresser), and TG (transgenderist). Once you get past a whole new set of acronyms, the world you'll find is chockful of the same sorts of problems, feelings, and attitudes you'd find anywhere else.

The agonizing journey necessary for self-discovery in the trans-gendered world seems to add an extra layer of sensitivity and kindness to these people. They regularly receive death threats on the phone and on-line, and are often jeered at by "macho" men and teenagers. Reading through the posts, one college student wrote, "This stuff is sick!" Many other regular members of the community received an e-mail message from the "Church of Euthanasia," which stated, "Save the planet, kill yourself."

Some men come to find their true love in alt.transgendered. "Lee" posts: "I sincerely have an interest in transsexuals and/or TVs. I am an intelligent, professional person in my early 40s who once had an affair with a preop transsexual. I had never had any interest in a gay relationship, and considered myself completely straight. I would love to get another chance to meet someone like the lady I once met. However, it's not easy. We can respect your need for privacy and understand your reluctance to share this board." Lee hits a nerve. His post adds more fuel to the ever-burning fire on alt.transgendered about whether it is appropriate to post personals ads on the newsgroup. The posters battle among themselves in a long-winded exchange, undecided between starting a new group for personals called alt.transgendered.personals or just creating a specialized Internet mailing list.

Many people write seeking advice about everything from where to find the best surgeon, to how to lighten eyebrows, and to how to psychologically and emotionally cope with the challenges of this life-style. Others seek crisis advice on dealing with parents who have stum-bled across their stash of dresses when they swept under the bed.

As a woman growing up and living in a society that places a greater value on the face value of females than their inner virtues, I won-der about a man's decision to become female. After all, most people think that men have an infinitely easier time in society than women. Some of the male-to-female postoperatives report a similar experience. "Samantha" posts: "As a two-year postop MTF, I can attest life as a woman is no bowl of cherries. Initially I tried to live the cultural mainstream view of what a woman is. For a while, I tried so hard that I was practi-cally a cartoon of what the American woman is 'supposed' to be. Finally, I began to get a clue and actually understand what feminists had been saying about sexism. For a while I overreacted to the other extreme, and practically became a lesbian separatist. Now, I'm simply being the woman I am without defining myself with someone else's standards."

The people who post on this message base are unique individuals worthy of respect, or at the very least, compassion and civility. We all have our own unique journeys in life, but people with gender identity issues have a much higher mountain to climb than most of us. You can learn a lot about the perils of prejudice and hatred by reading through the posts in alt.transgendered and learn about the power of self-esteem and self-direction in battling those wars. A male-to-female preop posts: "On the way home from the doctor, a bunch of men driving past me shouted out of the window 'DYKE' at me, as loud and offensively as they could. Somewhere here there's a little poetic justice. They were trying their hard-est to insult me, and they ended up complimenting me by mistake!"

Usenet Personals

The Usenet personals are where humanity cries out to be loved. Forget about the personals you've read in your local newspaper, which usually read as one long ad from the same person: a straight man or woman who likes long walks on the beach, moonlit nights, gourmet dining, fine wine, and nights by the fireplace. Yeah, and who doesn't! But people on the Internet tend to get a little more outrageous, honest, and provocative with their personals postings.

Here are the personal newsgroups you'll find on Usenet:

alt.personals

alt.personals.ads

alt.personals.bondage

alt.personals.misc

alt.personals.bi

alt.personals.spanking

alt.personals.fetish

alt.personals.big-folks

alt.personals.poly

alt.personals.fat

alt.personals.spanking.punishment

The generically named alt.personals and alt.personals.ads are the most popular of the personals newsgroups, generating thousands of new posts per week. The remainder of the digital social meeting meccas cater to fringe interests and draw significantly fewer posts. However, alt.personals.bondage, while not as popular as the generic all-purpose personal ad stomping grounds, draws hundreds of new posts each week.

The D/s community is so specialized in their kinks that they formed several personal ad offshoots to serve specialty interests with alt.personals.fetish, alt.personals.spanking, and alt.personals.spanking.punishment. Two newsgroups devoted to spanking? Interestingly, the only difference between alt.personals.spanking and alt.personals.spanking.punishment is that the latter discriminates against those seeking same-sex punishment spankings!

As on the rest of the Internet, men outnumber women significantly in the digital personals areas. A female can expect to receive hundreds of e-mails in response to her post. On the other hand, a male is lucky if he gets one actual, bonafide reply. Amidst the thousands of posts on alt.personals, it's unclear how any one advertisement could stand out. Straight men have told me that they simply troll through the headings looking for any personal posts from females, and relegate their reading to those select posts.

Behind the anonymity of my America Online account, I decided to test the newsgroup to see if any men would diligently sort through the thousands of posts to read my ad. I wrote a mild-mannered ad stating that I was a New York City–based "32-year-old woman with red hair looking for a male companion." There was nothing overtly sexual about my ad. In fact, it was downright boring and the only descriptive feature was the mention of hair color. I logged on to my America Online account a few days later to find I'd received over 200 pieces of e-mail! I received endearing notes from college students who had just seen *The Graduate*, and were seeking to live the fantasy. I received several notes from couples eager to add a lone female to their entourage. Another AOL member read the ad and responded with a GIF image of him naked and at full mast. Another man sent an enormous Valentine created in ASCII art.

A few weeks later, I created a male identity on America Online and posted a similarly generic ad seeking female companionship. I didn't receive a single reply. I came away with a profound respect for men and the heavy cross they bear in the social scene. If you're looking for love, it helps to be female, but if your genes say otherwise, it probably helps to be interesting. Heterosexual men cannot afford the luxury of posting boring personal ads on the Internet if they're serious about generating a decent response rate.

Personal ad found in alt.personals.fetish

Subject: The Mail-Dominant Lifestyle
Message-ID: <3Ø1ndm$bjf@news.u.washington.edu>

The Mail-Dominant Lifestyle

I am a thirty-seven years old man, with seventy-four years of experience with the Mail-Dominant Lifestyle, including prenatal and past life experiences. If you are a submissive-postal yearner seeking a Dominant-Mail to fulfill her postal longings, reply immediately, via Federal Express. I will train you and bring you those magazines with the tiny perfume inserts and will enable you to experience the various aspects of monthly electricity bills.

However, you must be patient. I have received many responses to my postings, and, I may be awhile responding to your query, but then you know what postal speed is like. It may be an even longer while before I come up with a new ad.

Personal ad found in alt.personals.poly

Subject: Polyamory in S.F. Bay area

The thing about polyamory is that you can be looking for more than one thing. I am, I would hope you were too. A person life has room for a lot. If you are a couple, or a lone women, if you are looking for a one, or just a sex-fun-person, or if you are kind of looking for something deeper and longer lasting that does not rule out the others. There is room for all in the open world of Polyamory.

I don't believe that nonmonogamous means uncommitted. I don't believe that you have to be rich to be different, or that older means you have to give up looking and take what everyone else wants, and seems to think you should too.

My name is Patrick, I am a 40 year old man living in Palo Alto. There is no one special person in my live right now, but if there every is to be, she will be a women who loves science fiction and sex. All else is open to being defined as we go along, with the help of friends and lovers, needs and wants.

If this sound like you, or you just want to be friend with someone who thinks like this my email box is open.

Personal ad found in alt.personals.bi

To: alt.personals.bi
Subject: married man seeks same for email

Seeking a married man who wants some release by exchanging hot email. Could be about anything. your wife, yourself, another guy... i find that marriage is great but can get stagnant if you don't generate some excitement. i'm very open with my wife but i need something else. to get stuff off my chest without being judged. my fantasy is to have a best friend who i would want to include in bed with me and my wife. or just me. or just her. and be able to talk openly about it and explore things without shame.

reply and we'll see if we're thinking about the same things.

alt.romance

If you're a love-starved college student who is a whiz at computing but a washout in relationships, you probably would feel at home in alt.romance. The group's FAQ is broken into three lengthy parts, the sum total well over 100 pages. You'll find tidbits like the following in the FAQ: "With rare exceptions, women are not offended if you make a pass at them, as long as it's done with some amount of taste. In fact, after a fairly short period of time, women draw an important conclusion if you *don't* make a pass. And that conclusion is that you're not terribly interested in being more than a friend." Hey, but don't some of us women just assume he's gay?

Anyone over 30 will probably feel as old as Methuselah after spending any time reading posts in alt.romance. College students post sappy, love-struck poems about their Internet lovers which begin, "I feel my heart slipping away to someone miles from me. I reach to hold it back but I cannot grasp it." Lonely college students post, "I'm sitting here in front of my computer screen, feeling blue and lonely. I'm away from home for the first time in my life." "Scott" posts that he's an "EX-TREMELY lonely college student whose search for someone special has not gone as planned. If there's a female out there on the Net that just wants to talk romance, e-mail me please."

It's been a very long time since my peer group discussed "the good-night kiss." "What should a guy do to get the kiss started and under what circumstances is it OK to throw a girl a nice kiss?" asks "Bob." "Henry" responds, "You could avoid kissing altogether and end the evening with a nice bow with a flourish, a good handshake, a wave good-bye, or kiss your finger and touch it to her lips." A bow with a flourish at the end of date? Henry has perhaps been watching too many 1940s movies?!

The conversation on alt.romance is sweet, romantic, and idealistic. If you're a high school or college student in need of friendly advice and a warm digital shoulder to cry on, alt.romance is like the older, wiser brother or sister we all wish we had growing up.

Here are some popular acronyms you'll find on alt.romance:

GF	Girlfriend
ILY	I Love You
IMHO	In My Humble Opinion
IMO	In My Opinion
LDR	Long Distance Relationship
LJBF	Let's Just Be Friends
MOTAS	Member Of The Appropriate Sex
MOTOS	Member Of The Opposite Sex
MOTSS	Member Of The Same Sex
POV	Point of View
RFA	Romantic Fire Association

RP	Romantic Partner
SO	Significant Other
YMMV	Your Mileage May Vary
WPTH	Weight Proportional To Height

Usenet Picture Files

Although you'll find picture files scattered throughout many of the text-driven, sexually oriented Usenet newsgroups, you'll find photos—and only photos—on these binary newsgroups:

alt.binaries.pictures.erotica

alt.binaries.pictures.erotica.d

alt.binaries.pictures.erotica.bestiality

alt.binaries.pictures.erotica.blondes

alt.binaries.pictures.erotica.cartoons

alt.binaries.pictures.erotica.d

alt.binaries.pictures.erotica.female

alt.binaries.pictures.erotica.furry

alt.binaries.pictures.erotica.male

alt.binaries.pictures.erotica.orientals

alt.binaries.pictures.supermodels

alt.binaries.pictures.tasteless

alt.binaries.pictures.utilities

alt.sex.pictures

alt.sex.pictures.female

alt.binaries.pictures.erotica.bondage

alt.binaries.pictures.erotica.fetish

There are the standard *Playboy* and *Penthouse* magazine type of images available—in fact, overzealous men, unconcerned about copyright issues, frequently upload home-scanned images of their favorite Bunny or Pet for everyone to enjoy. Few people seem concerned about copyright or privacy issues at all. Hell hath no fury like a scorned man. Many a scorned man, burned in romance, has uploaded personal, private nude photos of an old girlfriend as an act of revenge.

If you sat back and let your mind roam free, and asked yourself, "What are the kinkiest sexual acts in the whole world?" whatever your list is comprised of, be it men in diapers masturbating, or a woman giving a dog a blow job, you'll find a photo of it somewhere within the above-listed newsgroups.

Before uploading or downloading images to any of the binary newsgroups, it is highly recommended that you first read some of the binaries' FAQs. I highly recommend reading Jim Howard's (deej@cadence.com) alt.binaries.pictures FAQ, Parts 1, 2, and 3 for a comprehensive education on the art of uploading, downloading, decoding and encoding techniques, and picture formats. This FAQ is posted every other Monday on alt.binaries.pictures, as well as on alt.answers and news.answers. The most important rule to follow is to obey the commandment that picture newsgroups are for pictures only. Discussions should only take place on the picture discussion groups. If you find a binary picture file group listed with a solitary "d" at the end, that means the newsgroup is for discussion (text posts) about the picture group.

How does one know what pictures are appropriate to post? According to Jim Howard: "The basic answer is anything you'd like to see here yourself! However, if you got the file from some FTP (File Transfer Protocol) site that was announced over the Net, don't bother posting it. The odds are that everyone and their dog already have it, and we need to be careful about wasting bandwidth. If you're unsure whether there is interest in it, just post a short message saying 'I have this file, mail me if you want a copy.' If 500 people say they want one, post it, but if only one bozo from Outer Mongolia wants it, it's a sure bet the picture has already made the rounds!"

The most common standard for binary file transmission is the UUENCODE standard, with Apple's BinHex running a distant second. UUENCODE converts binary files into plain text ASCII files that can be handled by the mail system. You will need a version of UUDECODE in order to view anything downloaded from the Net. You can find a version of UUDECODE generally available on alt.binaries.pictures.utilities. If this newsgroup or your system does not have a version of UUDECODE available, you can get one via anonymous FTP from bongo.cc.utexas.edu in the gifstuff/uutools directory.

The most common type of picture is the GIF (Graphic Interchange Format), which is usually denoted with a *.GIF* file suffix. JPEG

(Joint Photographic Experts Group) is another popular image compression picture format, denoted with a *.JPG* file suffix. To view a picture of a particular type, you need a viewer suited for the configuration in question. GIF and JPEG viewers are very popular all over the Internet, as well as available on 99 percent of all on-line services, from your local bulletin board to commercial on-line services.

The following table lists many of the most common file types for pictures or compression formats for different systems. This information may be useful as a quick reference to the enormous amount of file types you may encounter on the Internet. Decompressors or viewers of less popular system types exist on some systems.

ARC	ARChive (many OS's support) - compressed file(s)
ARJ	Another archive format - compressed file(s)
BMP	Windows and OS/2 BitMaP picture file
CPT	Macintosh CompactPro compressed file
DIB	Windows and OS/@ BitMaP picture file
DL	Animated picture file (system independent for those with viewers)
FLI	Animated picture file (system independent for those with viewers)
GIF	Graphics Interchange Format - system independent picture file
GL	Animated picture file (system independent for those with viewers)
IMG	IMaGe - picture file
JPG (JPEG)	Joint Photography Experts Group (system independent for those with viewers)
LSH	Amiga LSH - compressed file(s)
MAC	Macintosh MacPaint - Macintosh Picture file
HQX	Maxintosh BinHex - encoded file

IFF	Amiga Interchangeable File Format - Amiga file interchange (used for many types of binary data). If it contains a picture file, then the picture is either an ILBM (InterLeaved BitMap), HAM (Hold-And-Modify), DHAM (DynaHAM) or SHAM (Sliced HAM).
IM8 (RAST)	Sun RASTer file - Sun picture file
PCX	IBM PC Paintbrush - IBM picture file
PICT	Macintosh QuickDraw PICTure - Macintosh picture file
PS (PSID)	Encapsulated PostScript/Post Script Image data - printer-ready text/picture file.
RAW	RAW RGB - 24-bit system independent picture file
SEA	Macintosh Self-Extracting Archive
SHK	Macintosh Shrinkkit - compressed file(s)
SIT	Macintosh StuffIt - compressed file(s)
TGA	TrueVision TarGA file - picture file
TIFF	Tagged Image Format File - 24-bit system independent picture file
UUE	UNIX UUEncoding - encoded file
XBM	X windows Bit Map - UNIX/X windows pictures file
Z	UNIX LZQ "compress" - compressed file(s)
ZIP	MS-DOS ZIP - compressed file(s)
ZOO	MS-DOS ZOO - compressed file(s)

Generally, people who post pictures include a brief, one-sentence description to generate interest like "Blonde women with huge breasts performing fellatio on horse." I bet that got your attention, right? In the same manner, thousands of picture posts compete against each other for downloading attention. The catchier the keywords, the more popular the file initially is.

Users subscribe to the picture newsgroups just like any other Usenet newsgroup. If you want access to the pictures, your site must subscribe to it. Talk to your news administrator about carrying the pictures hierarchy if it is not available at your site.

The pictures newsgroups are not the only source for pictures. Other pictures can be found in archives reachable via FTP (File Transfer Protocol—a program for transmitting files over the network). To use FTP, you need access to a computer with the FTP program and a network connection. FTP sites are generally not UUENCODED, so files must be transferred in binary when getting nontext files. For more detail on FTP, refer to the "how to find sources" posting periodically available on comp.sources.wanted, alt.sources.wanted, and news.answers. It is also possible to get anonymous FTP sites via e-mail. Send e-mail containing the text "help" to ftpmail@decrwrl.dec.com. However, a word to the wise: Anonymous FTP sites for erotic pictures are almost like vaporware. They exist for a minuscule amount of time and then seemingly vanish overnight. People frequently post requests for erotic FTP sites all over the adult newsgroups. According to Howard: "This is considered very poor form. As the sage once said, 'Revel in your illusions, don't share them.' The effects of sharing your illusion in this case always result in your illusion being rendered non-existent."

Afterglow

I had a dream last night. I was at a cocktail party where all the party guests hid behind ornate masks, drank truth serum in place of wine, and proceeded to reveal their deepest, darkest, innermost fantasies and desires. I listened to everyone's bold proclamations with a mixture of awe and bewilderment. I arose, and realized the dream was a metaphor for my months spent poring over the posts on Usenet's adult side.

Usenet offers a sense of tremendous empowerment in many ways. No matter what the question, someone out there in digital Internetland has the answer. No matter how odd you might think you are, you can find your cybertwin, as well as the rest of your long-lost family tree, somewhere in Usenetland. The Net is replete with an infinite assortment of human behavioral, sexual, and interactive experiences and information.

I don't know if I'm experiencing "afterglow" or monitor burnout, but I'm dizzy from "meeting" the parade of disparate souls alive and posting on Usenet. The incredible parade of humanity can make the average person's head spin while filling it with infinite knowledge about every conceivable lifestyle. Although this section of the information highway may have material some of us may be troubled by and wish to censor, ultimately, this would be a disastrous course of action. Rather than prevent the dissemination of information, we should attempt to use the information responsibly. One doesn't become a pedophile by reading about pedophiles, but the knowledge gained by learning about their rationale is invaluable. Knowledge is power, and the power to protect a child may come from understanding what makes a pedophile tick.

The Usenet is a subculture of its own, with complicated social structures and mores that are inconceivable to outsiders. "Mistress Minx Kelly," an artist, writer, and devotee of alt.sex.bondage, sums it up best:

> Imagine, if you will, a virtual arena, a place of infinite proportions where we can make anything happen and where we are only limited by the depths of our intellects. We can be chaste maidens or the Whore of Babylon as our moods shift. We can be our wildest dreams, or we can just be ourselves. Most of all, cyberspace is about self-definition. Every word we type, every hint or idea we share is solely of our devising. No one imprints us with rigid patterns to follow, or hopeless expectations to fill. We show people our inner selves with little reservation. We define ourselves as wee see us, and all our images are self-imposed. Imagine a world where how you see yourself is how others will see you. Imagine walking into a room and having people listen to you before they form an opinion. Imagine having a social setting free of prejudices and opinions based solely on appearance. Imagine a liberation from stereotypes of skin color, weight, or dress code. THIS is the arena we seek, and that we have founded. Usenet is our playroom, our newsroom, and our living room.

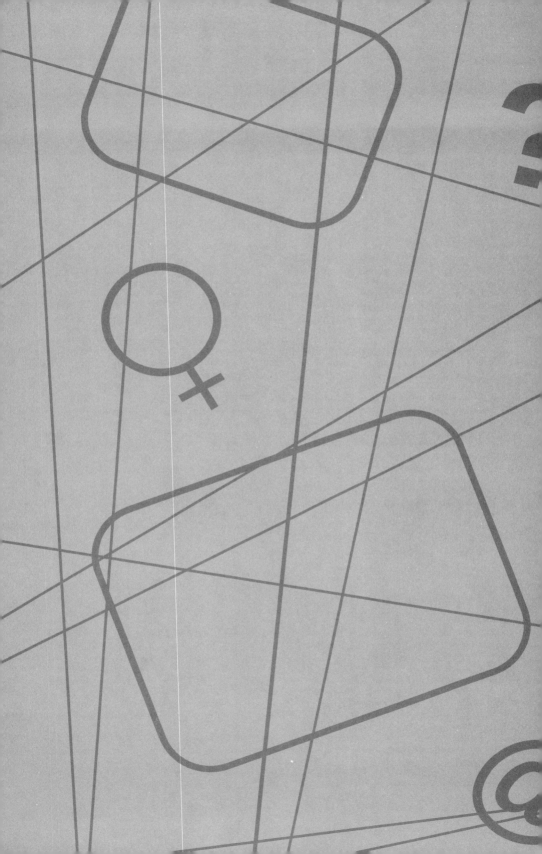

The world's largest digital party line

The champagne glasses clink as toasts herald the start of a grand new life. Marsha and David have walked down the virtual aisle, among scores of well-wishing cyberfriends, and tied the proverbial knot. After months of active on-line courting, Marsha and David decided to make it official by having an Internet Relay Chat or IRC wedding. They sent out wedding invitations to their IRC friends, and 100 "attended."

"My net life is a whole other life for me," states Marsha. "I have a great big net family who all really care about me. It's great on IRC. I get all the stuff I was missing from my own family. David and I even have a daughter on the net." Off-line, Marsha is a college student in Canada, and David is an East Coast–based accountant. They've never met in person, or even spoken on the phone, but their on-line married life has deep off-line significance. "I love him very much," swoons Marsha. "He said he might come up to see me sometime soon. We want to see if this relationship can work in real life." However, appearances can be deceiving on IRC. As almost everyone adopts an alias, female handles are often really male, and sometimes vice versa. David might find that Marsha possesses as much testosterone as he does.

IRC is a multiuser chat conference area similar in concept to a CB radio, offering hundreds of channels on which you can talk in real time with others all over the world. According to the Undernet IRC FAQ written by Mandar M. Mirashi, "Channels on IRC are dynamic in the sense that anyone can create a new channel, and a channel disappears when the last person on it leaves." If you're a transvestite looking for like-minded souls or a single looking for one-handed typing climaxes, or if you just want to take a dip in the communal hot tub, there is an active channel teeming with hundreds of users waiting for you. According to IRC's FAQ, written by Helen Trillian Rose, IRC was originally created by Jarrkko Oikarinen in 1988. Since IRC's launch in Finland, it has been used in over 60 countries around the world. IRC is constantly evolving, so the way things work one week may not be the way they work the next. No important international news stays local very long with IRC. The IRC "grapevine" gained international fame during the 1991 Persian Gulf War when updates from around the world came across the wire, and thousands of IRC users gathered on a single channel to hear these reports.

The IRC habit can be a tough one to shake. Many college students, feeling lonely and isolated on campus, log on to IRC for hours every night, receiving a virtual fix of digital socialization. "Joseph," a college freshman at a large Midwestern university, found acceptance on IRC. "I'm not a very adept conversationalist in real life. On-line, I find it a lot easier to open up and make new friends." Living away from home for the first time in his life, Joseph regularly suffers pangs of loneliness and turns to IRC for a socialization fix. "I sometimes spend up to six or seven hours on-line at a time," explains Joseph. "I feel the most lonely at night, and it is nice to know that there is an instant community of people to talk to at any hour." Joseph "met" a young woman on IRC, a California-based freshman, whom he has fallen head over heels in love with. "I'm almost afraid to meet her in person," says Joseph. "After spending three months on-line talking for hours at a time, I feel like I really know her. However, I also supplement our on-line time with a rich fantasy life about what real life would be like with her. If reality bites, I can't go back to the fantasy."

According to Elizabeth Reid's 1994 thesis, "Cultural Formations in Text-based Virtual Realities," which is circulating on the Internet,

> Much of the opportunity for uninhibited behavior is invested by users of IRC in sexual experimentation. The usually culturally enforced boundaries between sexual and platonic relationships are challenged in computer-mediated circumstances. Norms of etiquette are obscured by the lack of social context cues, and the safety given by anonymity and distance allows users to ignore otherwise strict codes regarding sexual behavior. Conversations on IRC can be sexually explicit, in blatant disregard for social norms regarding the propositioning of strangers. This type of behavior is often referred to as "net.sleazing." Perhaps because the majority of users of IRC are in their late teens to early twenties, since the Internet primarily serves educational institutions and students, thereby sexual experimentation is a popular Internet game. Adolescents, coming to terms with their sexuality in the "real world," find that the freedom of "virtual reality" allows them to safely engage in sexual experimentation. Ranging from gender-role switching to flirtation to "compu-sex," IRC provides a medium for the safe expression of a steady barrage of typed testosterone.

Depressed adults, getting over nasty breakups or simply lost in a bad case of social malaise, often overdose on IRC activity. There is always someone to talk to on IRC, and people quickly become loyal to their favorite channel. Others enjoy the thrill of deception. "Mention to one person you're 300 lbs., then say that you're 150 lbs. to another, and the results are hilarious," states Steve. "It's thoroughly amusing to gauge how an altered identity in terms of sex, physical description, interests, mannerisms, etc., results in such widely divergent feedback."

IRC is a popular activity among college students, frequently acting as the catalyst to forge friendships between students all over the world. However, sometimes people log on to IRC and end up meeting the boy next door. That's what happened with Nicole and Polaris. They were attending the same school, but never met until they became friendly on IRC.

Nicole takes issue with some people's belief that IRC devotees are socially inept "nerds."

> I think the vast majority of IRC callers are socially and universally conscious and aware that there are a variety of cultures and opinions beyond their own particular family, race, religion, university, etc. IRC provides a real-time discussion with other people around the globe, and a chance to talk to people you'd never normally meet and learn more about them, where they are, and what makes them think and feel the way they do. I've met pilots, actors, engineers, simply all kinds of people from all over the world. If there is one trait IRC denizens seem to share, it is a desire to experience people from completely different viewpoints. Sure, there are people who use IRC as a replacement for real-life relationships, but most IRCers (in my experience) use IRC to enhance "real life." It's not a replacement, just another dimension of life and experience.

Are there any general netiquette guidelines in place on IRC? According to Mirashi, there are several rules that people are encouraged to abide by. While the most widely used language over IRC is English, it is not the only one. When you join a channel, try to use the language that most people on the channel understand and use. Most channels frown upon obscenities or profanity. Using IRCII's /ON facility to automatically say hello or good-bye to people is extremely poor etiquette. An autogreet is a macro created by the user which will automatically say "hello," or whatever the person chooses the autogreet to express, to all people logging onto the channel. Mirashi believes that autogreets come across as insincere and interfere with the personal environment of each recipient. "If somebody wants to be autogreeted on joining a channel, they will autogreet themselves," jokes Mirashi.

"When you arrive at a new channel, it's advised that you listen for a while to understand what is being discussed. Joining in is encouraged, but never try to force a topic into a discussion that doesn't come naturally," advises Mirashi. "And refrain from flooding the channel with text. This can be extremely frustrating for people with slow modem connections and is likely to get you instantly kicked off the channel. Also, harassing another user with unwanted messages and comments is an IRC no-no as well."

The IRC is currently divided into a major and minor league. The mainstream EFnet IRC, (the term "EFnet" stands for eris-free net, a now-defunct Berkeley server) is increasingly overloaded and overwhelmed by new users; the Undernet is lesser known and smaller. The Undernet is maintained on a different network than EFnet, is much smaller, and was designed to enhance the overall space of IRC. The servers follow a much better server-server protocol, while maintaining the same server-client protocol. "The term 'Undernet' was suggested in jest by some of the original operators who started it. As time went by, the name stuck. Upon hearing the name, people often think that it's a net where something illegal goes on—which isn't quite the case," explains Mirashi. "On the other hand, the name also imparts a mysterious angle to the IRC net. On the whole, it's a very friendly net with an easygoing atmosphere. Most people are nice and helpful to newcomers."

The consensus among Undernet devotees is that this alternative IRC net is a "good thing." According to Mirashi: "Too much pressure is put onto the EFnet IRC due to the explosion of users it has gained. Many people don't ask if the EFnet IRC will survive, but when it will go. For this reason, the Undernet stands out as a good thing. It helps take the load off the EFnet IRC and prolongs judgment day, hopefully for long enough that a solution to its problems can be found."

Whatever part of IRC you're in, all of cyberlife is a stage, and no place is more theatrical than IRC channels "#Desire" and "#Hamnet" created by the Hamnet Players. An English "Stanley Kowalski" shouting "STEEELLLLL-AAA" to an actress in Tel Aviv? A New York City "Blanche" flirting with "Mitch" in South Africa? What's going on here? According to the group's producer, Stu Harris: "The Hamnet Players debuted the concept of Internet Theatre as a participatory performance art forum in December 1993 with a production of *Hamnet*, an 80-line version of *Hamlet*, which was repeated in February 1994 with Ian Taylor, of the Royal Shakespeare Theatre, in the title role. Shakespeare's 430th birthday was marked by the world premiere performance of *PCbeth*: an IBM clone of *Macbeth*, a 160-line pastiche which pioneered the use of visual images in the form of JPEG files."

The Hamnet Players enter their respective lines from all over the world, from London to Tel Aviv to New York City. True to the spirit of live theatre, Hamnet Playesr productions are prone to Murphy's Law. "The debut performance of *Hamnet* was interrupted by a thunderstorm which cut one of the producer's on-line access," states Harris. "The play had to be restarted after the producer logged back on via Taiwan."

"Actors are given their lines and cues by e-mail but no rehearsal is scheduled. Thus, no one but the production team will know the entire script until it unfolds on the net. Anybody with Internet access will be able to play the part of the audience for the events, and some may be offered roles spontaneously if technical difficulties prevent prime actors from appearing," states Harris. And there is no running out for *The New York Times* to check for a review. "Criticism and commentary is solicited during the 'cast party' held immediately following the performance."

Aspiring net actors can apply for roles in the current production of *A Streetcar Named Desire* without worrying about cattle calls and sending in their 8-by-10 glossies. Although past productions have involved formal casting calls, the *Streetcar* production is being cast by e-mail—first come, first cast.

Whether the action is pure theatre or soap opera, the dynamics of IRC live interaction are always original. In real life we can regulate and modify our human behavior by observing a wide range of actions— from nods, smiles, and tone of voice to eye contact and more. However, separated by modem lines, and possibly thousands of miles, IRC users have no direct way of observing physical reactions. Therefore, IRC users have developed their own form of emotional shorthand. "Emoticons," also known as smileys [:)], are omnipresent on IRC, as are acronyms. New emoticons and acronyms are created every day, and it is often difficult for the novice user to interpret the endless stream of characters. But the standard smiley :) is eternally popular and denotes pleasure or amusement, or is sometimes used to soften a sarcastic statement.

How do women fare in the male-dominated world of IRC? Mistress Minx Kelly, an on-line devotee, discusses the strength of IRC activity for women. "Women can explore other sides of our sexuality that are forbidden in real life. On-line, we can flirt and masturbate with other women, hot-chatting [the exchange of erotic dialog on-line] and expressing that hidden side of ourselves that even our closest friends don't know about. We must use our minds in hot-chat. Creativity is fundamental.

"Humans are always looking for a way to interact sexually and emotionally," explains Mistress Minx. "Cybersex allows us to do that without the pressure of 'putting out' or being overly concerned about socially acceptable body stereotypes. Some of us on-line women are gorgeous, and some are not, but all are intelligent, and must have at least enough intelligence to run a computer."

Is it morally correct to hot-chat within the confines of a monogamous relationship? Opinions from the cybersexual front differ. "Many men go on-line to search for extramarital sexual outlets," states Minx. "I only flirt or hot-chat with married men that I know have informed their wives of their actions, and who condone it. Otherwise I feel their actions are harmful to their union. In my own situation, my husband enjoys the wild times I have on-line. We can fuck and suck on-line, be anyone, in any time period we want, all without the dangers of sexually transmitted diseases. And as women, we are totally in control. If a man harasses us or tries to overstep his boundaries, we are only a hang-up away."

"Mark," a married, 34-year-old Silicon Valley programmer, views his IRC jaunts as total, unadulterated adventure, where truth takes a backseat to a good time. "I think anyone who thinks they're going to meet their soulmate on IRC is a diehard optimist, completely naive, or has never had a real life beyond their computer. I log on to IRC to play, and pretending to be something I'm not, like single, is part of the game. I'm here to flirt and stretch my erotic boundaries—all within the confines of my modem's reach—without hurting my marriage. Any woman who gets hung up on me, via our on-line lovemaking, truly has no life, and should seek professional counseling."

Many people report obsessive experiences with men and women they met via IRC. A young male college student, "Orinda" answered a personal ad from a young woman, Lisa. "To me, IRC is just a series of sentences coming over a CRT, nothing more, nothing less," states Orinda. "People out there who do get married, fall in love, etc., baffle me." After a series of discussions on IRC, Lisa asked to meet "Orinda" in person. "Immediately, she forced the physical intimacy side. She kept hugging me and touching me. After the get-together, she phoned me constantly. It was a difficult relationship to shake. She felt much more intimate with me than the actual friendship warranted. It was like she projected an entire, fully formed relationship onto our IRC time."

Some regulars on the alt.irc newsgroup are disgusted by the recent media flood of attention regarding Internet activities. A request I posted soliciting interesting personal IRC-related experiences elicited several angry posts, along with a flurry of interesting anecdotal experiences. "Orc" posted: "This fall isn't like any other fall. The cheap shysters, the terminally clueless, the survey takers, and the thrill-seekers are falling out of the woodwork like they've been gassed. If this is the 'information superhighway,' Clinton has a lot to answer for. Perhaps it will lose its thrill when the fortune hunters realize the natives are better armed than they are."

One man objected that I could even infer that a positive social real-life experience could ensue from an IRC courtship. "A couple of women I know in real life have gotten involved with men they met on the Net and have not been happy. In one case, a charming attractive woman, albeit a bit heavier than society deems desirable, was led down the garden path by a married man, after wasting months agonizing over the relationship. She is now engaged to another man she met on IRC who is already married, but claims he cannot locate his spouse. However, I enjoy the opportunities IRC provides for me to chat real time with people I know, and to sample opinions of those distant from me. But what passes for intimacy on the Net is wishful thinking."

Typing speed counts on IRC. People frequently maintain multiple conversations simultaneously, translating keyboard sluggishness to a limited IRC appeal. "Speed of response and wit are the stuff of popularity and community on IRC," writes Reid. "The IRC demands speed of thought—witty replies and keyboard *savoir faire* blend into stream-of-consciousness interaction that valorizes shortness of response time, ingenuity, and ingenuousness in the presentation of statements. The person who cannot fulfill these requirements—who is a slow typist, who demands time to reflect before responding—will be disadvantaged. For those who can keep the pace, such 'stream-of-consciousness' communication encourages a degree of intimacy and emotion that would be unusual between complete strangers in the 'real world.'"

The anonymous nature of IRC enables creative users to run wild with their imagination. While in our real life we're stuck with what God has given us, anything goes on IRC. No matter what digital costume we feel like slipping into that day, we always have a closetful of new clothes to choose from. It is possible to appear to be whoever you wish whenever you want. However, the uninhibitedness and total freedom have a price. Hostility as expressed in senseless flames and manipulative actions are damaging in any culture, on-line or off. "Anonymity makes the possibility of social punishment for transgression of cultural mores appear to be limited," states Reid. "Attracting the anger of other users of the system is a relatively unthreatening prospect—all that user needs to do is change his or her nickname to 'start afresh' with the people he or she had alienated." If only the government's witness protection program was so easy!

Whether the friendships and love relationships forged on IRC end up everlasting or fly-by-night, to quote the New York State Lottery's slogan: "You've got to be in it to win it." And for anyone who feels they *have* to be in IRC the majority of their day or night, alt.irc.recovery awaits. This Usenet support goup is targeted to IRC addicts, providing a haven for IRC junkies to converge in cyberspace to get over their respective habits.

"Ron," a college student posts, "It's been over a year in recovery now, and at least my backslides aren't so frustrating or so scary. But what do you do after you've had a small failure, and logged back on IRC?" "Greg" responds that the best course of action is to "send all your IRC friends e-mail telling them to rag on you if you ever show up on IRC again." Greg believes that negative feedback has its place in recovery, and even offers a monetary reward to anyone who spots him on IRC again.

Sometimes fellow IRC addicts are less than supportive. "Doug" belittles Greg's monetary reward method, stating, "If you have so little willpower that you need to offer your friends money to spy on you to keep you off IRC, you've got a much bigger problem than IRC addiction." "Jonas" rushes to defend Greg, stating, "Obviously, you are unaware just how addictive IRC can be. In the future, when Internet connections are as common as cable TV, IRC addiction will become a major problem in society. Just wait and see."

Some Widely Used IRC Commands and Phrases*

Command	Result
/help	Gets you help information.
/join # hottub	Joins you to "hottub" group. If you want to join another group, insert another channel name.
/msg <nick> <msg>	Sends private messages to person you specify. Only specified person will see this message.
/part #<channel>	Exits user from named channel.
/who is <nick>	Shows "true" identity of someone.
/list	Shows a list of all available IRC channels (this will take a few minutes to compile).
/list -min 20	Lists channels with 20 or more members.
/ignore user@host ALL	Ignores people who flood you or your channel with unwanted messages. To find user@host for person, do /whois nickname, or /who nickname. If you just wish to ignore messages from one person, you may do /ignore nick MSG. Use /help ignore for more information on this command.
/names	Shows nicknames of all users on each channel.

* All IRC commands start with a "/" and most are one word.

Some Widely Used IRC Commands and Phrases* (Continued)

/who #hottub	Shows who is in the "hottub" group currently.
/query <nickname>	Opens private conversation with another user.
/topic<some-text>	Sets or changes topic of channel user is on.
/quit #hottub	Takes you out of IRC.
/bye	Quits IRC.
/clear	Clears screen.
/away <some string of text>	Used when user does not wish to leave IRC but can't attend to screen for a while. Anyone who /msg's or /whois's that user will be sent message saying that he or she is away, with his or her explanatory text attached.
/mode #demo +p	Channel operator's option to change status of channel "demo" from public to private.
/mode #demo +m	Moderated channel.
/mode #demo +s	Secret channel.
/mode #demo +l 10	Demo channel is now limited to 10 participants.
/mode #demo +i	Demo channel is strictly invite only.
/mode #demo +n	No messages to channel "demo" are allowed.
/time	Displays time and date local to that IRC server.
/nick <some text>	Changes the IRC user's nickname.
/wallops <some text>	Writes a message to all IRC operators on-line. Useful if special technical help is needed with IRC.

* All IRC commands start with a "/" and most are one word.

Some Widely Used IRC Commands and Phrases* (Continued)

Pub	Public or "visible" channel.
Channel Operator	"@" before someone's nickname indicates he or she is channel operator. Channel operator has control over specific channel. First person to join channel automatically receives channel operator status. Channel operators can kick anyone off their channel for any reason.

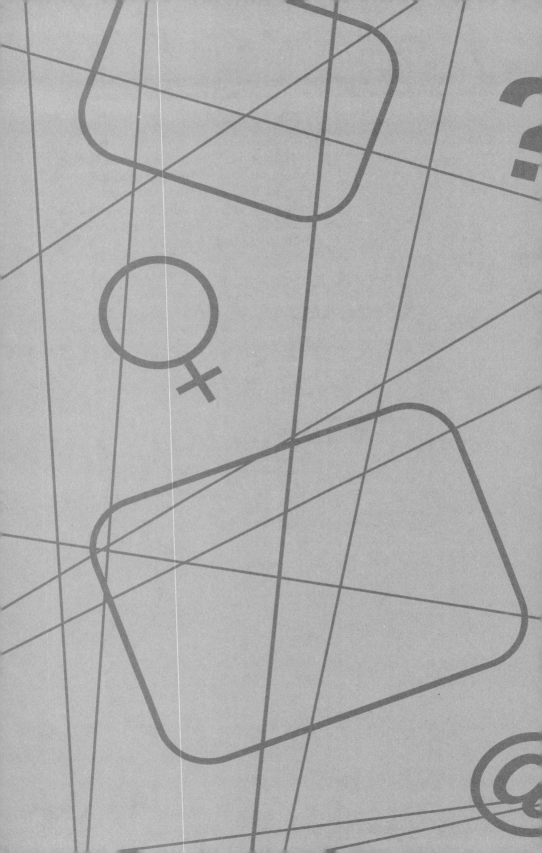

Are MUDs dirty or the best clean entertainment in cybertown?

Imagine a place where you can be anything you want to be, anytime you want. You can be a shining black knight armed for battle, an otter looking for trans-species sexual bliss, a fair damsel in distress, or virtually anything else the depths of your imagination can dream up. MUDs (Multi-User Dungeon, Multi-User Dimension, or Multi-User Dialogue), and their spin-offs—MOOs, MUCKs, MUSHes, COOLMUDs, Cold-MUDs, DikuMUDs, DUMs, LP-MUDs, MAGEs, MUSEs, TeenyMUDs, TinyMUDs, UberMUDs, UnterMUDs, and UriMUDs—are text-based, networked, multiparticipant virtual reality (VR) systems commonly found sprinkled throughout the Internet. It seems every day someone creates YAMUD (Yet Another MUD).

A MUD is a computer program, usually written in UNIX, that runs on a server that can be accessed over phone lines and is text-based. There are hundreds of different MUDs available on the Internet. All the other variations of MUDs, from MUSHes to MOOs, are part of the MUD "family" and referred to as MUDs as well.

The appeal of MUDs is really quite simple. Mudding instantly transports you into a fantasy land where you can be anything you want. It provides the ability to try on new roles and see how they fit. The 90-pound weakling can play the conquering hero, and the 220-pound body-builder can transform himself into the ultimate damsel in distress.

A MUD experience is a virtual reality session minus the goggles and special gear. Anyone who can Telnet on the Net can magically transport themselves to faraway lands filled with exotic characters and an infinite array of plots. Pavel Curtis, a programming language designer at Xerox's Palo Alto Research Center who created LambdaMOO as an experiment, describes MUDs in his paper "Mudding: Social Phenomena in Text-based Virtual Realities" as

> Network-accessible, multiparticipant, user-extensible virtual reality whose user interface is entirely textual. Participants (usually called players) have the appearance of being situated in an artificially constructed place that also contains those other players who are connected at the same time. Players can communicate easily with each other in real time. The virtual gathering place has many of the social attributes of other places, and many of the usual social mechanisms operate there. Certain attributes of this virtual place, however, tend to have significant effects on social phenomena, leading to new mechanisms and modes of behavior not usually seen in real life.[1]

MUD Terminology

MUD	Multi-User Dungeon.
MUSH	Multi-User Shared Hallucination.
MUG	Multi-User Game.
MOO	Multi-Object-Oriented.
SMUG	Small Multi-User Game.
Bot	A computer program that logs into a MUD and replicates human qualities.
Cyborg	Part man, part machine. In the MUD community, a cyborg is someone who uses their client to do some of their work by employing such tactics as auto-greets or an automatic response to trigger words.
Dino	Someone who waxes nostalgic about MUDs long since departed.
Furry	An anthropomorphic intelligent animal, i.e., an animal with human characteristics. Generally, furries reside in FurryMUCK.
Haven	On some TinyMUDs, there are flags associated with each room. The Haven flag is one of the more popular flags. When a Haven flag is set, no characters may engage in mortal combat.
Maving	According to MUD folklore, Mav is a TinyMUDer who accidentally left a colon on the front of a whisper, thereby directing a private message to the whole room. Mave now generally refers to any type of communicative typing confusion.
Player killing	The act of player killing is as varied as the MUDs themselves. On most combat-oriented MUDs, player killing is taken very seriously and is the modus operandi of the game. However, on most TinyMUDs, where there is little or no active combat, player killing is employed as a tool of emphasis, i.e., another player ticks you off, so you "kill" him or her as a dramatic gesture.
Spamming	To spam is to intentionally flood the screen with sentences, making it impossible to read anything coherently on the screen.

MUD Terminology (Continued)

TinySex   TinySex is libidinous, heated MUD banter and actions
                 which replicate sexual intercourse.

MUDs: Social and Adventure Opportunities

There are two major types of MUD environments available on the Net:
social and adventure MUDs. Social MUDs, including the TinyMUD/
MOOs and "Talker"-style MUDs (similar to a chat channel on the IRC)
are generally warmer and friendlier places than adventure MUDs. Social
MUDs don't wield the total control found in adventure MUDs. Elizabeth Reid, a doctoral candidate at the University of Melbourne, dove
into the world of MUDs and wrote a comprehensive thesis entitled "Cultural Formations in Text-based Virtual Realities," which is widely distributed on the Internet. "Players do not have to fight to gain points and
levels before they can build simple objects and create new areas of the
game universe," states Reid. "Novice players on a social MUD are able to
do these things. The rank of Wizard is not dependent upon gaining
points. The elevation to Wizard ranking is at the discretion of the Gods."

A longtime mudder, "Dan" explains that the social MUDs are
places where the object is to meet people. "Think of it like any other social gathering, except you can control the volume," Dan said. "There's a
common misconception that there is any one group of people that lives
on the MUDs. We see people from all walks of life, all professions, age
groups, etc. With the proliferation of companies offering access to the Internet, the Net has made major inroads into mainstream society."

How often does gender ambiguity surface in the MUD arena? According to Curtis,

> It appears that the great majority of players are male, and the vast ma-
> jority of them choose to present themselves as such. Some males, how-
> ever, taking advantage of the relative rarity of females in MUDs,
> present themselves as female, and thus stand out to some degree. Some
> use this distinction just for the fun of deceiving others, some of these
> going so far as to try to entice male-presenting players into sexually ex-
> plicit discussions and interactions. This is such a widely noticed phe-
> nomenon, in fact, that one is advised by the common wisdom to
> assume that any flirtatious female-presenting players are, in real life,
> males. Such players are often subject to ostracism based on this as-
> sumption.[2]

Marlene describes herself as "a blonde-haired vixen with the long, lean legs of a high-fashion model, a clear porcelain complexion, and dazzling green eyes." As you enter the drawing hall, she privately purrs in your ear, "My description is real, and I really dig women. Are you bi?" In reality, Marlene is Nick, a 22-year-old graduate student who spends up to six hours a day at his favorite virtual environment.

Curtis offers this theory about such posts:

> Some MUD players have suggested that such transvestite flirts are perhaps acting out their own (latent or otherwise) homosexual urges or fantasies, taking advantage of the perfect safety of the MUD situation to see how it feels to approach other men. While I have had no personal experience talking to such players, let alone the opportunity to delve into their motivations, the idea strikes me as plausible given the other ways in which MUD anonymity seems to free people from their inhibitions.
>
> Other males present themselves as female more out of curiosity than as an attempt at deception; to some degree, they are interested in seeing "how the other half lives," what it feels like to be perceived as female in a community. From what I can tell, they can be quite successful at this.[3]

Although nobody "knows you are a dog in cyberspace," to quote the famous *New Yorker* cartoon, no one truly believes you are a real live "girl" either. Curtis said that many female-presenting players are frequently (and sometimes quite aggressively) challenged to "prove" that they are female, while male-presenting players are rarely if ever so challenged. Curtis believes that because of these problems, many players who are female in real life choose to present themselves otherwise, choosing either male, neuter, or gender-neutral pronouns. However, even the neuter and gender-neutral presenters are still subject to demands that they divulge their real gender.

And just like the john who picks up an attractive streetwalker, discovers they have equal levels of testosterone, and kicks him out of his car in disgust, MUD players also find it difficult to interact with someone whose true gender has been called into question. "Since this phenomenon is rarely manifest in real life, they have grown dependent on 'knowing where they stand,' on knowing what gender roles are 'appropriate.' Some players (and not only males) also feel that it is dishonest to present oneself as being a different gender than in real life; they report feeling 'mad' and 'used' when they discover the deception," states Curtis.

Alex had a less pleasant experience with digital transvestitism. "Unfortunately, my first experience with falling in love on a MUSH happened with someone who was actually a man playing a woman, and I was too inexperienced and bought the act. It hurt a lot. I remember being saddled down with a migraine headache for hours after I learned the truth. However, I got right back up in the saddle, went back mushing, and I'm glad I did."

However, Andy has been playing a female character for over a year on a combat-oriented DikuMUD, and he feels his gender-bending experiences have provided a valuable peek into the female role in society. He confides that "it has been an enlightening experience. Sexism exists on a MUD just as it does in real life, and it has helped me to understand women better after having to experience just a small virtual sliver of what their real world is like."

Behind the safety of one's PC, MUD players sometimes form strong personal attachments to fellow participants. Sara, a devotee of a popular social MUD, states that her best friends are her MUD friends, all of whom she's never met. MUD romances are a phenomenon of the '90s. "On social MUDs, the most common action taken by romantic partners is to set up a virtual house together," states Reid. "They quite literally create a home, using the MUD program to arrange textual information in a way that simulates a physical structure which they can share and invite others to share. These relationships may even be virtually consummated through 'tinysex,'" an exchange of lusty thoughts and actions sometimes resulting in one-handed typing climaxes.

Like everywhere else in cyberspace, females sometimes face unwanted attention from males in the MUD environment. Pavel Curtis says that his female-presenting LambdaMOO players report a number of problems. "Many of them have told me that they are frequently subject both to harassment and to special treatment. One reported seeing two newcomers arrive at the same time, one male-presenting and one female-presenting. The other players in the room struck up conversations with the putative female and offered to show her around, but completely ignored the putative male, who was left to his own devices."

Imagine having wild, uninhibited sex with a brand-new lover, only to discover that the entire session was filmed, and the videotape circulated all over town. Unless you are a hard-core exhibitionist, you'd probably be very embarrassed. Similarly, some devious Romeos persuade unsuspecting newbies into engaging in "tinysex," log the proceedings, and post the orgasmic highlights in rec.games.mud, a popular Usenet newsgroup for MUD players. "I have to know a guy several weeks before I'll even think about engaging in 'tinysex,'" says "June." "A girlfriend of mine had her MUD sex session posted on Usenet, and the embarrassment drove her off MUDs. She made the mistake of jumping into bed, so to speak, before she really knew the guy."

"Flo," a 40-year-old female artist, was drawn into mudding by the lore of meeting new people all over the world and the adventure of seeing the programs and descriptions people dream up. Flo enjoys role-playing a female adolescent cat who chats about seafood. However, Flo said that "fending off guys in virtual reality is exactly like doing it in real life." During her first month mudding, she became friendly with a male character who invited her over to his virtual house for a virtual dinner. They sat on the sofa and he started "putting the moves" on her. She rebuffed his advances, proclaiming she was too young, but he persisted. Ultimately, they both confessed their real ages, and her male suitor began asking endlessly for real-life advice. "He told me he had no time to look for a real job, but when I looked him up in the game, I could see he'd been playing for over five hours. For a while, he was paging me every few minutes. He acted like I owed it to him to take care of him," Flo complains. Other male characters Flo has encountered simply move in for the sexual kill way too soon. "One of them even attempted to start having sex with me without any prelude."

The Revenge of the End of the Line MUD offers technical, as well as emotional, guidance for MUD couplings, announcing, "For those loving couples who wish to discover the joys of matrimony, the command to get married is 'marry <person>'. Both parties must do the command. We don't believe in shotgun weddings or polygamy here (though same-gender marriages are fine with us)."

"Rasmus" enjoys a MUD marriage with an Israeli woman. "If you're a man like me who finds it hard to meet women, you can be sure to find someone to talk and flirt with whenever you want. I have a very good relationship with my mudwife, and even send real letters to her. It possibly obstructs any 'normal' relationships but I've never considered myself 'normal.' I think many mudders are socially inhibited in real life. I know I am."

However, Rasmus is well aware that his mudwife is no replacement for the real thing. "I think of my relationship with her as a mutual daydream, with all its benefits and drawbacks. To some extent, you can shape an image of your partner, suiting your own needs. I feed on the melancholy and dissatisfaction of the relationship as well."

Human sexual pairings pale in comparison to the trans-species couplings found in FurryMUCK. FurryMUCK, on-line since October 1990, has grown to become one of the Internet's most popular social MUDs. All players who enter this domain are encouraged to "go fur it" by playing anthropomorphic beings and experiencing the ultimate beastly pleasures. You may meet a talking walrus sporting a beret and tuxedo, a unicorn who hails from another galaxy, or a lounge lizard who attempts to slither his way into your heart. The Captain and Tennille never envisioned "Muskrat Love" would one day be practiced by humans on FurryMUCK.

Elizabeth Reid has these observations on MUDs in her thesis:

> With adventure-style MUDs, such as the LP-MUD and DikuMUD programs, there is a strict hierarchy of privileges. The person with the most control over the system is the one running the MUD program. Known as the God, this person has complete control over all elements of the virtual world. Gods may create or destroy virtual areas or objects, and destroy or protect player's characters. The players, on the other hand, have very little control over the system. They cannot build new objects or areas and have no power over those that already exist. They can only interact with the MUD environment. They can kill monsters, collect treasure, solve problems, and communicate with one another. By doing these things, players on adventure MUDs gain points, and a certain number of points translates to privileges. Once a player has collected enough points, he or she may be elevated to the rank of Wizard. Wizards do not have the complete degree of control which is available to the God of the MUD. They cannot alter the MUD software itself, but they do have the ability to create and control objects and places within the MUD universe.[4]

Interestingly, some courageous women, although widely outnumbered by men, gravitate to the adventure MUDs, which are often billed as "hack 'n' slash" environments. A male college student and active MUD enthusiast notes that "women are definitely in the minority on combat MUDs, but in approximately even numbers with men on the socially oriented and role-playing MUDs." Even among all the slashing and dashing, true love sometimes rears its optimistic head. "I met the woman I love on a DikuMUD. We started off grouping together to kill orcs and dragons, then flirted, became friends, and when we met six months after first 'seeing' each other on the MUD, it was like we had known each other all our lives. She has since moved from Virginia to California to be closer to me," says "Andy." "We engaged in flirtatious foreplay a number of times, and when we finally had netsex it was fun, especially because we were becoming good friends at the time."

"Hevard," a habitué of GrimneMUD, a Diku-based MUD, enjoys the camaraderie. "On GrimneMUD, grouping is encouraged. If you group up with other players, you are better able to kill monsters. By playing you get to know other people, or rather the characters they portray, from all corners of the globe as they Telnet in. Mudding gives you a chance to redefine yourself. It is just like moving to another city. No one knows you, and you have the opportunity to create a new self."

The MUD community is fairly fluid, with new MUDs launching and closing every day. The only news as common as a MUD announcement is news about a MUD going out of service. rec.games.mud.announce is a moderated Usenet newsgroup where announcements of MUD opening, closing, moving, and related parties are posted. alt.mud is a general all-purpose newsgroup and the first newsgroup created to discuss mudding, but the activity level is low. Other general newsgroups include rec.games.mud, rec.games.mud.misc, and rec.games.mud.admin (pertaining to the administrative side of mudding). To keep abreast of what is going on in the specific communities, it is wise to take a gander at the related Usenet newsgroups such as rec.games.mud.diku (posts pertain only to DikuMUDs), rec.games.mud.tiny (posts pertain only to the Tiny family of MUDs), and rec.games.mud.lp (posts pertain to LP-MUDs only). Another excellent source of information is the three-part MUD FAQ, which can be found on alt.answers, news.answers, or archived at ftp.math.okstate.edu:/pub/muds/misc/mud-faq.

Some MUD veterans are chagrined about the recent upsurge in new members due to increased media attention. One old-timer groused that new users tend to ignore the written and unwritten MUD rules. Most MUDs provide very well-defined documentation that explains the MUD's rules, regulations, and methodology, and is must-reading for new users. "I've seen clueless newbies who stumble into a MUD asking where the tinysex is, or bashing homosexuals," said an experienced MUD player.

Other MUD loyalists reject the widely held notion, perpetrated in the press, that MUDs are so addictive that people quit school or their jobs. "The vast majority of MUD users finish school," states "Frank." "The people who *do* drop out don't do it because of gaming. Some people find structured education boring. And only a small percentage of the gaming population becomes obsessively addicted to mudding."

Edmond L. Meinfelder, a four-MUD veteran, wrote an article for his college newspaper on the virtues of mudding. He believes that the challenges put forth on MUDs cause people to learn on many levels. "The average chemistry student may have no understanding of computers, but have a passion for mudding," Meinfelder writes. "Because of this passion, it is quite likely this student will gain a knowledge of programming, leadership skills, and improved written communications. On the Internet, your race, gender, sexuality, age, and looks really don't matter. Your ability does."

Although no reliable MUD census data exists, it appears that the majority of MUD enthusiasts fall in the age 18–28 age range, are in college, or have college or graduate school degrees, and significantly more men than women participate. However, there seems to be a growing minority of young professionals in their late 20s, 30s, and beyond who are attracted to the medium. Given the strong emphasis on creativity and science-fiction plot lines, it is not surprising that science-fiction and fantasy fans are attracted by the world of mudding.

There are no absolutes with MUDs. You cannot assume that people who are into MUDs are social misfits. Nor can you assume that every woman into mudding looks like Shelley Winters. MUDs are what real life would be like if people stretched their imagination every day, and reached for the moon. MUDs require thinking and mental prowess. MUDs require that you study the "rule book," both official and unofficial, of your chosen domain. On one social MOO, a male character repeatedly asked all female characters if they would engage in phone sex. Amidst a chorus of complaints, the system's God stepped in and ousted the offending character. It's nice to know that God is alive and well and living in cyberspace. If only there were some omnipotent presence on the New York City streets to sweep away those offensive street characters who shout endless-loop choruses of "hey baby, baby, give me some of that" to all passing females, proving that New York City may be dirty but it ain't no MUD.

Notes

[1-3] Pavel Curtis, "Mudding: Social Phenomena in Text-based Virtual Realities." *Intertek* 3.3 (1992).
[4] Elizabeth Reid, "Cultural Formations in Text-based Virtual Realities." Ph.D. diss., University of Melbourne, 1994.

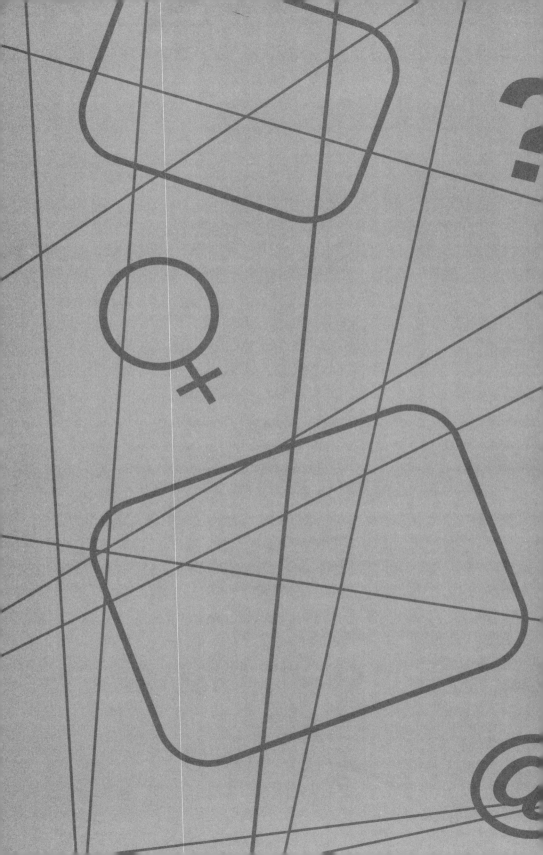

Epilogue: Respect

There is no reason to abandon off-line sensibilities and etiquette just because you are physically concealed behind a monitor, computer, and modem. Have some respect for humanity when you log onto the Internet. Here's what respect means to me:

R is for the **R**espect you should treat Net citizens with at all times.

Rudeness should not be tolerated on-line or off. Some people seek refuge behind the safety of their monitor, saying whatever they want, even if it is tantamount to character assassination. "Flamers" are incendiary on-liners who incite trouble with derisive commentary. The most effective way to douse the flames is to ignore them. Flamers enjoy rattling others' cages, but simply deplore being left alone in theirs. Ruin their day and disregard them.

Most flamers are simply doing their best to yank another's chain. While in real life, no one would stay in the same room with these offensive louts, in cyberspace they have a worldwide audience to annoy 24 hours a day. However, flamers beware: Sooner or later, we all recognize your e-mail address and immediately scroll past your flames without stopping, or simply add you to our respective killfiles, thereby never having to read from the likes of you again.

Keep in mind, however, that about 5 percent of the time, the incredibly vile posts you are reading are the products of unattended terminals. Many new Net citizens are college students with university accounts, and a popular prank is to log on to a fellow student's unattended account and say something hostile like "gay people don't deserve to live" in the alt.homosexual Usenet forum. The unsuspecting student logs on the following morning to find his e-mail box jammed with a gigabyte of hate mail.

∽

E is for the **E**diting, **E**dification, and **E**tiquette you will employ before responding to Usenet posts.

Edit Thyself   There is nothing more annoying than seeing a public post that begins with 100 quoted lines and ends with "I agree" from the respondent. Do Usenet readers get any significant bang for their buck by scrolling through a post they've already read just to get that terse two-word contribution? I think not. Ask yourself, "Do I have some knowledge to impart here?" before wasting valuable Internet bandwidth space. Send private e-mail to the author if you have nothing to contribute to the quality of the newsgroup.

Select efficient, economic, and polite words in public posts. Less is more on-line. Save verbose postings for your private, personal e-mail, and keep the public Usenet and IRC areas clean by depositing as little digital litter as possible.

Edification Enriches, Ignorance Detracts   Every day, newbies sign on to the Internet, eager to share their sagacity with the digital masses. While we all long to hear their pearls of wisdom, wouldn't it be nice if each new Net citizen took some time to read pertinent net documentation before asking questions that have been answered thousands of times before? For example, many of the 7,000 Usenet newsgroups have their own FAQ (Frequently Asked Questions) file. Newsgroups generally post the complete FAQ file biweekly, and they're also located in alt.answers or news.answers, two Usenet newsgroups that maintain FAQ files. Also, many FAQs are archived at rtfm.mit.edu, in the directory /pub/usenet/your.group.name.

Etiquette Is Everlasting   An appropriate response to a newbie's post of "how do I view these computer photos...all I'm getting is a bunch of assorted characters" is *not* "figures a (fill-in-the-blank-of-the-commercial-on-line-service-net-veterans-detest-this-week) customer is such a moron, doesn't it?" Wouldn't it be nicer if you simply referred them to the comprehensive FAQ on unencoding binary files?

～

S is for the **S**hort and **S**weet **S**ignature files that are candy to the eyes, rather than those unwieldy, 22-line ASCII art creations that make reading through any Usenet newsgroup as mentally depleting as reading *War and Peace* backwards.

If you feel you *must* impart your personal "signature" on the captive net audience, keep your signature to four lines.

～

P is for finding the **P**roper **P**lace to **P**ost. Currently, there are over 7,000 Usenet newsgroups catering to very specific interests and topics of conversation. For example, while the act of rape may involve sex, it is not appropriate to post discussions about it in soc.singles and alt.sex. However, it is suitable to discuss rape issues in talk.rape. Similarly, a post on a volatile topic such as abortion would generally not be appreciated in soc.women, but would be welcomed with open arms in talk.abortion.

Before contributing to any newsgroup, read it thoroughly and get a sense of what is and isn't being discussed. Each group has its own style and unwritten rules about what is acceptable. Learn these before posting and find out if the newsgroup created an FAQ, and if so, read it!

～

E is for the Education and Enlightenment available on the Internet. It is hard to find a topic that has not been comprehensively covered somewhere on the Internet. However, if you have knowledge on a particular subject and would like to share it, the Internet is always looking for material!

Learn how to best surf the Internet to serve your needs. By utilizing Gopher and World Wide Web (WWW), the individual user gains access to the full resources of the Internet. Gopher displays a set of resources on the Net as menus from which the user can select. Exact Internet addresses are not needed—all users have to do is select an item from the menu, and they're there. Many browser-type personalities prefer tapping into the WWW, commonly used with Mosaic software. Rather than using menus, WWW uses text, with each page of text containing specially marked phrases (pointers) that lead userd directly to the resource being discussed. Users choose their own path through a document, jumping from resource to resource without even knowing which Internet computer they're on.

~

C is for the Control needed to prevent excessive Cross-posting. Is it really necessary to send the same message to over 7,000 newsgroups? Think very carefully before cross-posting your message to more than one newsgroup at a time. A personal ad that appears only in alt.personals will have greater success and suffer less flaming feedback than one that also appears simultaneously in alt.sex, alt.sex.wanted, alt.sex.first-time, and so on. However, sometimes it does make sense to send the same message to a few related newsgroups. If so, be sure to redirect all follow-up discussion to one particular newsgroup, so people interested in following the subject can find it. You can do this by adding a follow-up header line, along with a mention in the body of the article, stating which newsgroup you've directed all further discussion to go.

~

T is for the Tolerance all Net citizens should have for everyone who lives on-line, no matter what their lifestyle, race, religion, or creed. If you don't have the maturity to interact peaceably with the international Net community, *please* don't log on to the Internet.

INDEX